EXIT-EXISTENTIALISM

A PHILOSOPHY OF SELF-AWARENESS

EXIT-EXISTENTIALISM
A PHILOSOPHY OF SELF-AWARENESS

KENT BACH
San Francisco State University

Wadsworth Publishing Company, Inc.

Belmont, California

For Claire

ISBN 0-534-00309-5
L. C. Cat. Card No. 73-82997
Printed in the United States of America

1 2 3 4 5 6 7 8 9 10—77 76 75 74 73

Contents

What This Book Is About

Was Socrates right when he said, "The unexamined life is not worth living"? In order to disagree with him, you still have to examine your life. Besides, even if he was right, it doesn't follow that the examined life *is* worth living.

Was Camus right when he said, "Beginning to think is beginning to be undermined"? There's only one way to find out.

Asking basic questions about yourself can be painful. Suppose the answers hurt or there aren't any. You may wish to return to the garden of ignorance and innocence, but by now it is too late. The trap of thought is sprung.

Fortunately, as Camus observed, "We get into the habit of living before acquiring the habit of thinking." And for most of us, there are enough daily distractions to keep us going once we've acquired that habit. So to be realistic, we shouldn't overestimate the difference that thinking makes. Nevertheless, this book is based on the assumption that it does make some difference.

The thoughts in this book are reflective not only in the Socratic sense (of examining life) but also in the sense of being about thought itself (thinking about thinking). I use "reflexive" to mean the latter. The reflexive quality of consciousness is the basis of the quest for meaning and the idea of oneself. The process of examining reflexiveness is itself reflexive. As you get into it, you may find this labyrinth of echoes and mirrors to be teasing and dizzying. But don't give up too easily!

This book deals both in experiences and in concepts. Particularly experiential are the first three chapters, where an attempt is made to articulate by example and explanation a variety of feelings and experiences of meaninglessness and alienation that many of us have. Philosophers may be disquieted by the concreteness of this approach, and nonphilosophers may be skeptical of the attempt to put such feelings and experiences into words.

Despite the psychological observations and the sprinklings of anthropology and sociology, the book is essentially philosophical. For it seeks to outline the basic features of the experiences described and to analyze and connect the concepts involved in their expression. If a label had to be applied to this approach, it might be "analytic phenomenology." The approach is analytic because the nature of the concepts is spelled out, and phenomenological because these are concepts of experience, rather than theoretical ones.

I should mention how this book fits into the contemporary philosophical scene. Anglo-American philosophy, dominated by the methods of logical and linguistic analysis, is noted for its clarity and refinement but also for its technicality. It often gives the impression of being divorced from the traditional philosophical practice of reflecting on life. Some philosophers seem to find such reflection sentimental and unprofessional. Some refuse to call it serious philosophy, thinking it to be either not serious or not philosophy. Some are embarrassed by the question of the meaning of life, and others, on philosophical principle, brand that question "meaningless."

Existential philosophy, a European breed, has carried on the reflective tradition, using both phenomenological and literary methods. Unfortunately, it has developed a reputation, largely through Heidegger and Sartre (in his philosophical rather than literary writings), for obscurity and verbal mystery. Many analytic philosophers are sensitive to smog and, regrettably, seem to conclude that the philosophy of life is, by their professional standards, inherently sloppy and obscure.

There's no reason why philosophy can't be done clearly even on such questions as the meaning of life. That's what I try to do in this book.

Before giving a brief chapter-by-chapter picture, I want to mention a couple of snags to be avoided in reading this book. First, don't get fooled by the style. Its informality is meant to make the book easy to read, unlike many philosophy books. It may not be so easy to understand, however, and thoughtful effort will be necessary. Secondly, don't get hung up over the absence of academic appurtenances like footnotes and references to the views of particular philosophers. Certain ideas expressed here bear likenesses to ones associated with other philosophers, especially those labeled "existentialists." I make no attempt to delineate such resemblances. Instead, I have appended an extensive annotated bibliography that refers you to treatments of topics dealt with in this book. Hopefully, they make up for the many spots where I could have gone farther and deeper. The philosophically experienced reader should appreciate that philosophical neophytes, for whom this book is primarily intended, would get insufferably bogged down in technical details, however necessary these may be for accuracy and completeness. Here is a brief indication of the progression of chapters:

1. What can happen when you think too much and ask too many questions? You may lose all sense of meaning as you strip the world of all semblance of purpose. Reflecting on the fact of your own ultimate end, you wonder if anything can really matter. Things may seem comically or tragically absurd, or alternately both. Is it possible to escape the mental circumstances in which this sense of the absurd crops up?

2. However, escapism is an impermanent solution—nasty thoughts return. So another tack is taken, that a person can find meaning by finding something worth identifying with. He can, yes, but again only if he doesn't think too much. Reflection reveals identification as a most tenuous relationship. Indeed, the very act of reflecting undermines that relationship, by underlining one's separateness from everything else. Various examples of alienation illustrate this point.

3. There's always yourself to turn to, if you can't identify successfully with anything else. But there are obstacles to self-identification, as illustrated by numerous examples of self-alienation involving your actions, your feelings, your body, and your image. These difficulties raise serious doubt whether self-identification can ever fully succeed, whether any idea you have of yourself can be fully accurate and up-to-date.

4. There's a reason for this. It has to do with the sort of thing you are, which is that you are not a mere thing. After all, you are conscious, indeed self-conscious. But what is it that you are self-conscious of? What is this Self that you seemingly refer to, automatically and confidently, every time you say "I"? The more you think about it, the harder it is to isolate and identify. And yet what could be more familiar to you than yourself? Part of the difficulty has to do with the reflexiveness by which you are self-aware. By being reflexively conscious, you are always a step ahead of yourself.

5. Being a step ahead of yourself, what you are is always indefinite. Therein lies your freedom—what you are is not what you have to be. The world's silent indifference to what ought to be and what you ought to do about it leaves it all up to you. Well, some of it anyway, for the ideal of total control is a chimera. Fulfilling your possibilities doesn't always mean controlling them. Part of them are unpredictable experiences that can occur any moment. With that in mind, there's no point in forcing the future to spite the present.

Reflection is the recurrent theme of these chapters. It is what is being done in them, and it is what they are about. A striking feature of the whole reflexive process is found in its cyclical (or dialectical) character, in its persistent ability to create its own barricades and then to break through them.

The Hollow Whole 1

It is not how things are in the world that is mystical, but that it exists.

Wittgenstein

Where Have All the Meanings Gone?

Being alive is one thing; being aware of it is another. Can you recall the first time you realized you were here? I recall when I did. I wondered what in the world I was doing here. I could make no sense of it. Don't get me wrong: I was terribly glad to be here, but why I was here I hadn't the foggiest idea. Even then (I was young, ten maybe) I questioned the popular religious notions of why we're here, and I was willing to accept no substitutes. Here I was, through no fault of my own nor anyone else's. I knew enough biology to deny even my parents the credit for me. They may have wanted a baby, but they had no idea who it would be. What's more, the odds of the particular sperm fertilizing the particular ovum that produced me were less than one in a billion.

I'm glad to be alive, as I said. That's more than someone else I know, who entitled his memoirs, "Why Was I Born, or, Who Can I Kill to Get Even?"

I have no complaints, personally anyway. I haven't been hit hard by disease, poverty, war, or injustice. Millions have. So what's my complaint? None, as I just said. I have no specific problem, just a general one. I'm aware of being here—for no reason and only for so long.

No matter when you realized you were alive, you realized, too, that you were alive before you realized it. By cosmic standards, you hadn't been alive for long, maybe, but longer than you could remember. You know also that you won't be here for long. And when you think about this, it bothers you.

That's putting it mildly. When I think that the universe has been here practically forever and will continue likewise, I feel rather small. But then I reflect on the peculiarly human qualities that distinguish me from everything else known to me except other people, and then I don't let the vastness of the universe bother me so much. Most of it is space anyway, and the rest, merely combinations of particles.

In thinking of humanity, particularly of its few thousand years of so-called civilization, I feel swamped by the tide of history. Little that has happened is my doing. Little that will happen will be my doing. Others may do a little more or a little less (grains of sand vary in size). Sobering, yet liberating, is the thought that history is nothing but the cumulation of people's acts. I am one person, neither more nor less, just like you, and that's all anybody is. Societies, cities, institutions, and organizations are composites of people, people like you and me, and nothing more.

You might get the idea that although I respect people, I don't have much respect for the world in which they (we) live. I don't. Sure, its magnitude and complexity amazes me, but I don't read anything into it. It is, and it is the way it is. Nobody made it that way. Nobody cared that it was that way until it long since had been. I'm glad to be here, but grateful to nobody. I see myself as but another component in what is (in this part of the universe) the most advanced stage of a lengthy process of mindless geobiochemical developments, each stage of which is more improbable than the previous. Only after the fact can we entertain the idea that somebody planned it that way.

I don't disrespect the world, either. I just accept it for the unlikely thing it is. It isn't going anywhere. It hasn't come from anywhere. Quite the contrary. The world is precisely that in which things are coming and going, among them, ourselves.

This "scientific" view of the world is a relatively new outlook, considering the historical prevalence of all sorts of religion and myth. To primitive man, the world was rife with meaning. The world made sense and everything in it made sense. At least it made sense within the context of the mythic system that he and his fellows happened to live under. A mythic system is a unified coherent picture of things by which all humanly significant natural phenomena are integrated into the supernatural. Acts of men correspond to acts of gods. The human role in maintaining the scheme of things consists in observing practices and rituals that please or appease the forces that be and that recreate the patterns of yore. In such a scheme of things, the literal and the symbolic converge. Meanings aren't conventional attachments to things, as our meanings are attached to words. Meanings are *in* things. The sun is the sun god. Things reflect their mythic archetypes. Events are acts, not occurrences. Sacred objects and holy rituals are not mere tokens and gestures. They are embodiments and reenactments.

That was the way it was—a wholesale view of the world fully and unquestioningly held by one's fellows like oneself. It wasn't a matter of mere belief. Such a world view determined how the world *looked.* It defined what was there, not what was merely thought to be there. Therefore, any person or any people who didn't see things that way weren't mistaken but deluded.

A primitive mythic system played the joint role of theology, science, ethics, and ideology. These modern fields are, of course, separated from each other and abstracted from experience. A mythic system was integrated and concrete. In one fell swoop it organized the phenomena of birth and death and everything before and after and in between. Seasons and stars, droughts and diseases, terrors and territories all fit into the system. The people whose system it was were unaware of it. Rather, the system was how they were aware of the world.

Over the centuries, there has evolved a highly complex division of mental labor. Religion, science, ethics, art, and politics connect at the fringes. Or they overlap without being tied together. In either case, there are loose ends. More fundamental is that experience today is fragmented: the personal is separate from the social, the perceptual from the conceptual, the spiritual from the theoretical. For me, what I feel in the privacy of my own head may have little to do with my actions in everyday social situations. My perceptions of things have little to do with my knowledge of them. For example, my awareness of my own body has nothing (fortunately) to do with my knowledge of physiology. And, of course, my concern with why I am here and what it all means is not helped at all by my accumulation of scientific knowledge.

Science is wonderful but spiritually barren. It makes the world make sense, but impersonally and piecemeal. To me, unlike to primitive man, things and events are not laden with personal and holistic meaning. Everything that is just happens to be, despite all the fascinating relationships discovered and imagined by science. Scientific explanations make the world make but relative sense—they always take something for granted. Science cannot explain why the world makes scientific sense. It cannot explain in ultimate terms why we are here. For example, an evolutionary theory of life doesn't explain the existence of the matter from which life emerged. And a cosmological theory of the origins of the universe must ultimately content itself by saying,

"That's the way things were." Not only can science not explain in ultimate terms why we are here, science is silent on what we should do about being here.

Modern religion has difficulty picking up where science leaves off. First of all, religion is but one among other fields. It is not a unified whole and a whole unifier like a mythic system. Moreover, as dogma, it is something merely to be believed, not to be lived. People who really live their religions often have great difficulty communicating with others, and vice versa. We may regard them as fundamentalists or fanatics. They live not an ordinary, integrated life with society, but as cultists or missionaries. Finally, modern religions suffer from competition with each other and with science. As a result, they become watered down and "demythologized." They are all thought of as saying the same thing, as being merely symbolically different from each other and as not really competing with science at all.

Where does all this leave a person? Either you accept some religion on faith (that is, with no reason), or you reject it. That's assuming you think about it. Many people never bother to examine their beliefs, content as they are to believe what their parents taught them to believe and afraid to think otherwise. Naturally, I am assuming that anyone reading this book has done at least a little thinking.

As I mentioned earlier, I did a little thinking when I was ten. I have accepted no religion since I can see no reason for accepting one. All the arguments for dogmatic religion, especially those for the existence of God, have been butchered time and time again.

I know I sound dogmatic here, but after all, the burden of proof is on the believers. Some of them adopt the medieval *"Credo quia absurdum"* ("I believe because it's absurd"), but lack of a reason doesn't strike me as a good reason to believe. If a choice must be made, I'll adopt God's nonexistence as a working assumption. If I am mistaken, I hope He is not offended by my demand for evidence. (Many believers seem to think that God is offended by atheists. Is He overly proud or merely insecure?)

I can sympathize with people's need for religion, but to me, their acceptance of it is wishful thinking, if it involves thinking at all. I have little sympathy for those who embrace a watered-down version of religion, who interpret its texts "symbolically," and who partake in its rituals "culturally." If they cannot accept it intellectually, why fool around? "As-if" religion strikes me as a self-deceptive exercise in futility. If you can't take hymns and psalms literally, you might as well face the music.

The trouble, of course, is that there is little comfort in a world constituted by the mindless, inexorable workings of matter and energy. If that is all the world is, it is not exactly the sort of place to call home. And it is equally hard to think of the world as God's waiting room. The world just happens to be and we just happen to be in it. Love it or leave it.

Can Anything Really Matter?

You may not like my attitude, but I am just trying to face reality. To find my outlook objectionable is no objection to it. I'm trying not to take things for granted. That means pulling the rug out from under myself. I don't think I'm riding a magic carpet through life. Are you?

If my attitude bothers you, it is probably because you think that without myth or religion nothing can matter whatsoever. That's it, isn't it? If the world makes no sense to me, except scientifically; if I attribute no purpose to it and hence find no place for me in it, then nothing can possibly matter. Therefore, you're telling me, my life can have no meaning to me. And my death can be nothing but the curtain to the charade. That may be what you think I must think, and maybe you think the same thing yourself. And maybe you try to forget that that's what you think.

The fact is that many things do matter to me. At this moment of writing, these words and these thoughts matter to me. Their meaning to you matters to me. At other times other things matter: music, chess, family, friends, food, sex, peace, and sleep. These things and others matter to me at different times and in different ways. Some things are more important than others; some occupy me more than others. Some conflict with the rest more than others. And I am sure that whatever your values and interests happen to be, the same could be said for you.

Still, you might wonder, how can these things really matter to me? For if I see the world as a vast array of mostly mindless activity, then these little pockets of purpose in my life and in yours cannot amount to anything. If the world as a whole has no meaning and purpose, then the isolated meanings of this and that cannot be tied together. They are but passing fads and fancies. And if, moreover, I treat death as the end, then the things that matter from moment to moment can have no lasting value. For momentary pleasures and the life they pretend to enrich must come to an end. All they have in common is their ultimate futility.

What you're saying to me (and perhaps to yourself) is that with such a bleak and barren perspective on the world and on life as a whole, nothing *should* matter. In other words, if anything does matter to me, I am only kidding myself about my outlook on life. I think there is some truth to this.

Before explaining why, let me state what I think is involved in your suggestion that nothing should matter. You are assuming, so it seems to me, that all the little things that matter in life must somehow fit into an integrated whole, perhaps in accordance with some ultimate purpose or some ultimate principle of meaning. That is, there must be unity to the diversity of things that matter. Furthermore, you seem to be assuming that since these diverse things are fleeting, what ties them together must be permanent. Therefore, if the things that matter in my life cannot be unified somehow into something lasting, they cannot ultimately matter at all.

Now, the question is, why should I grant these assumptions? Why should things have to hang together and be lasting in order to matter at all? It seems to me that they should only so long as I, or anyone who shares my perspective, maintain the mental condition of considering the world and life as a whole. That is, if you are going to focus your attention not on what is happening right now and not on what you are doing right now but on the cosmic context in which these events occur, then it is no wonder that the demands of unity and permanence prevail. Once you adopt an eternal viewpoint and focus not on this or that event but on everything, then indeed it is impossible for every little bit to count unless it fits into something ultimate and eternal.

I mentioned before some of the things that matter to me. Each doesn't matter to me all the time, at least not consciously and actively. When my attention is on one of them, that thing alone is what matters then. The others matter only when I focus on them. However, when I stand back from the particular activities and situations that make up the variety of my life, when I look at my life as a whole, then I am no longer in the situation in which any of the things that matter to me matter. Now, in this reflective moment, I am contemplating them all at once. I am recollecting the past and anticipating the future—not just experiencing the present. Or rather, I am looking at my life outside of time, from an astronomical distance where I can see it all at once, not a bit at a time. From that standpoint, when I am not consciously engulfed by any one of the things that ordinarily matters from time to time, each one of those things seems a puny particle. This is something like the experience of looking from the top of a tall building at the people scurrying like tiny insects through the streets of the city. Their movements seem pointless.

Similarly, when I adopt the cosmic perspective, I feel engulfed by the vastness of space and time, and by the number of things therein. Even to focus just on my own life, but as a whole, swamps my consciousness. All the little bits compete for attention, but none is mighty enough to catch it. This is a case of what today is called "information overload." We might even call it "cosmic shock."

Have you ever been in a restaurant with an interminable menu and suffered from overchoice? I mean being unable to decide on anything particular because there is far too much to choose from? The problem is not just making a decision. After all, you could simply close your eyes and point, thereby picking at random. There is also the problem of trivialization—the sheer quantity of items makes each one seem insignificant in the company of the rest.

On the previous page, I admitted that if things matter to me, then I must be kidding myself about my outlook on life. I must be pretending (to myself) to hold an impersonal, "scientific" view of things. I admitted this then but I didn't explain why. Now I can.

To have a view of life as a whole requires assuming a global perspective. As we have just seen, for such a view to be full of meaning rather than devoid of it, there must be some principle of unity and permanence. If for me there isn't, how can things matter to me?

The answer is simple. Things matter to me precisely when I am not in the state of assuming a global perspective. They matter to me when I am involved with them specifically and oblivious to the rest. What I am kidding myself about, then, is not what my outlook on life is but the relevance of my outlook to my life. Every time I look at things from a global perspective, indeed whatever I am doing loses its meaning and fades into a wisp of triviality. But when I am involved in something, my outlook on life as a whole doesn't enter in. And when it does, I am no longer involved in what I am doing.

I would be kidding myself if I pretended that my outlook on life were irrelevant to my life. After all, whenever I have this outlook, what I am doing dissolves before my very eyes. The relevance of my outlook is not that it renders everything meaningless automatically and absolutely. Rather, it does that only when it comes to mind. These moments are part of my life, but only part. The rest of the time I can forget them.

When something matters, it matters; when it doesn't, it doesn't. These are important truisms. When, from the global perspective, everything that matters from time to time is supposed to matter all at once, nothing matters. Each thing is wrenched from the experiential context in which it normally matters. Instead, it has to compete with everything else. Each thing becomes trivial and arbitrary. Meaning, then, is what something needs in order to matter when one takes the global perspective. In its own context, something doesn't need meaning to matter. When I'm involved in it, it simply matters. It cries for meaning only when I'm reflecting on it, in the rather larger context of the cosmos. Only then is that cry unanswered.

Vanity Fair

Now that we have put this gloomy global perspective itself in perspective, let's take a look at it, recognizing that it needn't be chronic. What we are looking at, if you haven't yet labeled it such, is the absurd sense of life. The ingredients of the absurd emerge from the vantage point of too much perspective: (1) The impersonality of the workings of the universe clashes with the personality of human endeavors; (2) the universe has no apparent purpose, although it dwarfs and thereby trivializes the purposes that people find for themselves; (3) from so far away, things look roughly equal—their differences dissolve; and (4) seen against no background, the universe appears mere happenstance.

How indeed can anything in particular be significant if nothing that exists must exist? The whole world is a contingency. It might not have been. Still, it is pretty impressive, even if construed as nothing but occasional matter in occasional order.

Obviously, I am assuming that there isn't (or wasn't) a God who created the whole ball of wax. You might think that were there such a Being, the world would have a Purpose. If so, then I could value whatever conforms to that purpose. But then I ask, why should what matters to God matter to me? The absurdity of a God-created universe is no less than the absurdity of an uncreated one. From my point of view, God's existence, if indeed He happens to exist, is no less arbitrary than the existence of the world itself. Either way, here I am, thrown into a world not of my own choosing.

Another point about God and His Purpose: why should God have a purpose? Why should He need one? After all, He's not the one obsessed with purpose. I can't seem to justify my own purposes, but why should I demand a Higher Purpose to subsume my own under? If I made this demand I would fail to recognize that if anything should matter to anyone, God or otherwise, something should matter to me. This lesson is hard to learn and easy to forget. Many go through life without a purpose of their own. That includes slaves, wives, soldiers, and workers. I mean those of them to whom nothing matters unless it matters to somebody else, whether master, husband, government, or boss. (This is one form of alienation that we'll look into later.) For now I insist: if anything should matter to anyone, something should matter to me, and not because it matters to someone else.

In the global perspective, however, it is difficult for anything to matter to me. For it is then that the overall meaninglessness emerges. This philosophical sense of absurdity occurs in me often when I observe others. Right at this moment I see outside my window an old man tending his garden. Now his wife has joined him. They spend much time caring for their ephemeral flowers. Ignoring the beauty they sense, I am struck by the utter futility of their efforts. Their flowers bloom briefly, soon to wither away.

Almost every day I drive on the freeway. There are thousands of other drivers and passengers, each going who knows where. I sometimes wonder what difference it could possibly make where anyone is going or whether he makes it. That so many of them are in such a rush only underscores the gap between the magnitude of their intentions and the triviality of their fulfillment. Of course, such realizations don't prevent me from getting upset if the traffic grinds to a halt or my car blows a tire.

Sometimes I perch on a hill overlooking the whole city. As I contemplate the incredible complexity of this socioeconomic arrangement, this network of places to live, places to work, places to play, and places to shop, and the maze of roads and the signs and lights that show the way; as I contemplate the fact that some are working, some are sleeping, some are loving, some are dying, I think of the dust from which it all began and into which it all will ultimately return. This Ecclesiastical reflection is nothing new. All is vanity still.

When I become overwhelmed by the feeling I have in contemplating these towering trifles, the feeling turns coat completely. For I realize it is my feeling, not its object, that bothers me. And then I realize that all these people or almost all of them are normally oblivious to such reflections as mine. They go on their merry way or suffer their petty pains, reap their hollow harvests or succumb to their dour defeats, without being overwhelmed by the perspective of the whole. Suddenly they strike me as silly, even ludicrous. They are part of a huge joke, which consists of one part absurdity and one part my consciousness of it. Then the perception of the joke of it all gets mixed with the tragic sense. They don't mix well, and the feeling is like a pendulum swinging between sorrowful compassion and amused contempt.

The tragic irony of the life of others, of the cosmic drama itself, is not bypassed in my own life. For my own life is where the real problem is, for me at least. My exuberance, when I am exuberant, is mine, but so is my depression, when I am depressed. My own feelings and moods are not merely objects of my consciousness but states of it. Thus, they cannot be shut out but at best shut off. This goes especially for the sense of the absurd. How to shut it off, if that is what should be done with it, will be deferred for now. I haven't yet finished describing this sense of the absurd.

Isotopes of Absurdity

"It's all a joke!" "Somebody's putting me on."
If there is a God, He pulled one helluva fast one. And if there isn't, it's a joke that nobody played. In fact, it is a joke precisely because nobody played it.

The joke of life is that most people take it so seriously. They don't get the joke. I'm sure you've been told a joke you didn't get. Maybe you didn't even realize the person was telling a joke. And then, suddenly, after the conversation had veered in another direction, you see it. You have a genuine "Aha!" experience. You laugh in delight and feel painlessly stupid for not having understood it immediately. "How silly of me," you think, and you laugh again.

The joke of life is a different kind of joke—one that nobody gets immediately. You have to take life pretty seriously at first. You had to have made some sense of it all. Sooner or later, if you've thought long enough, you begin to see that this "sense" makes none, and if you aren't too hungry or too sick, you laugh heartily at the thought that life doesn't make sense and isn't supposed to. Why should it?

Once you see the joke of life and you've got your laughing out of the way, what next? The joke is stale, but the fact that made it a joke remains—that everything, as a whole, makes no sense. People plan for future yesterdays. They live with purposes perhaps forgotten, but founded on the fantasy that their lives have meaning. Do you feel contempt for their groundless designs? Or do you envy them for responding in illusion to the proud prod of purpose? Whatever you do, you have your own outlook on life to deal with.

"It's all a game."
That's a good way to look at it when the joke wears off. Games define a little world of their own and make no pretense to a meaning larger than themselves. You can take them lightly or

seriously, but any meaning they possess is temporary. When the game is going on, you can be wholly involved in it. When it is over, you can feel the joy of victory or the agony of defeat or just the exhilaration of having played the game.

There are as many different ways of viewing life as there are different games. But they all have in common the idea that like a game, life has no meaning beyond itself. They don't necessarily require winners and losers, and they allow for seriousness as well as levity. They even allow for players who take the games with ultimate seriousness.

There is just one problem with this analogy. Games occur within the context of life. They last for a certain length of time, and then they're over. But if life itself is a game, it is one of a kind. There are no rematches. It has no finish that can be looked back upon. It has no winners, only born losers.

Most of the players in the game of life don't realize that it is a game they're playing. But that, of course, is why life struck you first as a joke and now as a game.

Life is a funny kind of a game, then. You have no choice which game to play, only whether or not to keep on playing it. Sleep is the only time-out, death the final gun.

Perhaps you're getting sick of this "life is a big game" or "it's all a joke" nonsense. "So what" is your reaction. "So what" is another way of dealing with the absurd. Nothing really matters anyway. Everything is the same as everything else.

The "so what" attitude is an attitude of total indifference. No difference makes any difference. Any enthusiasm for something can be premised only on the illusion that something will come of it. Any depression about misfortune can be based only on the illusion that positive fulfillment was really possible. Any strong emotion, one way or the other, imputes importance that simply can't be there. It is not a mere acceptance of fate—"that's the way the cookie crumbles"—but recognition that even what one's fate is doesn't matter. The cookie crumbles.

Impassive indifference seems a most regrettable trait, however objectively justified it may be. Something is lacking in a life of indifference, its justification notwithstanding. But illusions are not easy to recover.

You need to have had an illusion in order to become disillusioned. Illusions come in many shades. Seeing through them varies in difficulty with the illusion and with its victim. We ask the most basic questions when we've seen through our respective illusions. Perhaps we realize what the question is when the illusion no longer answers it. As we hopelessly seek an answer, the thought gradually sinking in that none is to be found, but only fabrications, we feel alienated from things, from others, from institutions. People seem like puppets, organizations like farces, and objects like obstacles. When nothing means anything, life is at best a game, at worst a bore. What others find vital, we find trivial. Their passion is our lethargy.

When the sense of absurdity is fresh, ironic views of life are possible. Whether it is all a joke or all a game, or even if it is a worldwide tragic drama, it is still something. But when the pointlessness of it permeates deeply enough, sheer boredom may result. Now you might say that even if life has no point to it, at least it is not a drag. You might suppose that anyone who is just plain bored with life has a metabolic problem, not a metaphysical one.

It is not so simple as that. For one thing, people with this chronic sense of boredom needn't be spending years in prison or on an assembly line. Quite the contrary, they may have lived years of exceptional excitement, doing all those things that others can scarcely imagine doing. The thrill seeker or the Don Juan may have spent years without the frustration of a moment's disappointment. But finally, as he reflects upon it all for the first time, he realizes that it adds up to nothing.

Thrills and delights come and go, but they don't accumulate. Now that our reflective hedonist realizes this, he knows that the next satisfaction will no sooner be gained than lost. It is reflection that disturbs him, but once he thinks, he's through. Everything, he now realizes, is more of the same, a repeat performance, a rerun. He has exhausted all the variety that is the proverbial spice of life. The tedium is the message.

Such a person, you might say, needs a new spark. If his once prodigious vitality is sapped through self-reflection, perhaps he needs a change of scene. Surely there is something he's never cultivated. No doubt there is, but from his point of view, such opportunities are merely distractions from the lately realized truth. He is wise to these diversionary tactics. He has been caught in the act and can no longer return to the scene of the crime. The crime was living.

Suicide is a possible answer. Why continue living if life has lost its charm, or never had any? If there is no reason to live, then that, surely, is a reason to die. Simple logic, isn't it? The conclusion, however, doesn't follow. Otherwise, I wouldn't be sitting here writing this. I know there is no reason to live. After all, life leads to nothing but its conclusion. I just happen to like being alive, even when it's boring. You just have to learn how to make do with boredom, but don't ask me how you should do it.

I don't have any objection to living *per se,* though pain and suffering are not to my liking, nor to anyone else's. I don't happen to have too much of either, and I would be grateful for that if there were someone to be grateful to. I am not that depressed by the suffering of others. Do you know of anyone who is contemplating suicide just to relieve himself of the overwhelming burden of compassion for others? Fortunately, the more general the compassion, the more diluted it becomes. I can't say I am in love with life (that would be an exaggeration) but I can't complain either. So why put an end to it? Since I am not undergoing any excruciating and unending agony, why should I kill myself? Being bored occasionally is not sufficient reason. Being bored chronically is another problem, but imagination is its solution. Though I don't have a reason to live, I don't have a reason not to. Life doesn't require a reason. Terminating life does. Maybe this is a gross rationalization. Maybe I am simply afraid of death. No wonder that suicide is out of the question for me.

Death's Honesty

Everybody seems to fear death, but what, exactly, is frightening about it? It's not the pain of dying, for most people survive greater pains. Besides, a painless death is fearful nonetheless. The fear seems to have little to do with what happens after death. To be sure, some people still believe they'll burn in hell, but most of those who believe in a life after death should, you'd think, look forward to it. And if death is regarded as less than a dreamless sleep, namely nothing, then the answer given by the ancient Roman poet Lucretius should suffice: "When I am, death is not; when death is, I am not. Therefore, death is nothing to me."

If death were only that, it would be nothing to me. The problem is that I am aware of it before it occurs. Moreover, I have no idea when I am going to die. People who do know when they will die either seem to feel relieved or live it up until the final moment comes. It is more difficult to resign yourself to a death that is always at or below the horizon of time.

People tend casually to treat the fear of death as a case of fearing the unknown. But what is unknown about death? If death is a state of sheer nothingness, of no longer being and of never again to be, then what happens after death is known all too well. Perhaps it is the indefiniteness of its moment of occurrence that makes death so terrible to people, when they think about death. (Being led to the gallows or to the gas chamber is another experience entirely.)

The fear of death is not like the terror of being subject to a great and immediate danger, such as a wild animal or a violent psychopath. It is a fear of something inevitable, not immediate, and final. The thought of one's ultimate end is a reminder that whatever one is and whatever one will become will not remain. Death is an uncompromising attack on one's dignity. It renders everything puny. When one's death is in mind, nothing deserves serious attention, impassioned desire, or lasting ambition. People who think big haven't looked beyond the meager scope of their ambitions. The thought of death is a reminder that everyone is essentially the same: a helpless corpse-to-be.

Traditionally, death has been a promise or a threat of things to come. Or just part of the cycle of life. It has been conceived of as a moment of transformation or of transmigration. To me death is the end, period. For people to whom death defiance is a way of life, whose greatest thrill is challenging death, the meaning of death undergoes a peculiar twist. Instead of rendering everything meaningless, death is the source of meaning. Everything else is the boredom between the acts. On going back up to the high wire after his troupe's fatal Detroit accident, Karl Wallenda, the leader of the Flying Wallendas, put it, "To be on the wire is life. The rest is waiting."

Is the life of death defiance sheer madness or existential heroism? The judgment is left to you. The point about this way of life is its implicit acknowledgment of the relation of death to the significance of things in life. It is a way, perverse or not, of responding to death's threat to render life utterly inconsequential. Defying death is an attempt to conquer death by either holding it in contempt or beating it to the punch.

Death entered this discussion from two doors. First, death is the only alternative to life, and therefore it seems to be a possible answer to a life with no meaning or a life without a reason for continuing. We saw, however, that no reason for living is no reason for dying. The other way in which death came up was as the damper to anything meaningful or worthwhile in life. In passing, we looked at both the fear and the defiance of death. Now I wish to ask whether death is the source of the absurd or whether it only seems to be.

All along I've talked as if the finitude of our lives, the fact of death, renders everything in life insignificant. True, it succeeds in doing this only when we adopt the global perspective on things, but it is only from this standpoint that questions of ultimate meaning arise in the first place. It seems that the thought of death is enough to reduce the loftiest ambitions to triviality, since their fulfillment can never give lasting satisfaction. On the other hand, why should life be interminable in order for anything in it to be worthwhile? It need be only so long as the thought of its termination keeps nagging. Transience is significant only from a long-term perspective.

Moreover, it is not just the transience of mortal life but the transience of the things within it that counts. Even if life lasted forever, still the experiences and accomplishments at different moments within it would be brief. You could still be obsessed with the meaning of life. You might even be shocked by the fact, given the eternity of life, that there would never be the time when everything could be added up—there would always be more. Death, then, is not the source of the absurd.

Thinking Too Far

Next, I'd like to consider what makes possible this realization of the absurd, and then I'll try to see if there is any way to eliminate it or transcend it.

The sense of the absurd results from failing to answer the question of the meaning of life. It is reinforced by the recognition that there is no answer, that is, no positive answer. And this recognition results from the observation that any attempted answer takes something dubious for granted and perhaps even begs the question. People who accept some positive answer don't really understand the question in its full generality. Or, in trying to answer it, they don't look far enough. If they did, they would see that the answer they accept is subject to the very same question it pretends to answer. Thus, if a God or some elaborate cosmology is supposed to explain the existence and meaning of things, what explains the existence of God Himself or whoever are the principals in the cosmology? This last question often fails to get asked. To continue asking is sooner or later to give up hope for an answer. The next step is to see that there was no step to be taken in the first place.

Seeking the meaning of life requires a little dissatisfaction and the ability to ask questions. It requires reflective thought—the kind of thought that looks on life as a whole, not on this or that to the exclusion of everything else. Today there are many thinkers whose thoughts are corralled into narrow fields. They take much for granted, including the value of what they're doing in their field and the legitimacy of the fence around it. To take nothing for granted is to raise the most basic questions and to doubt our capacity to answer them.

What does reflection on life involve? It requires looking at life as a whole, not just on what is happening right now, but on life's duration. It requires abstracting from the individual differences between my life and yours and generalizing to the life of anybody.

Everybody is aware of the past and of the future, at least to some extent. Some people are more "time conscious" than others. While some may live almost wholly in the present, others may be living in the future or in the past (or both). Time consciousness may be short-term or long-term and it may shift from one to the other. Individual acts involve short-term time consciousness, plans and schemes long-term. Some people live solely for the sake of the future; others survive on nostalgia. Whatever the scope and whatever the direction of a person's concerns, they extend only so far. When your finger hurts badly, nothing else matters, then. When you've just met the woman (man) of your dreams, nothing else matters, then. When you're trying to adjust your TV set, or when you're seeking the presidency, or when you recall your first love affair, nothing else matters, then.

A person's consciousness is oriented in time, differently at different times. In particular, concerns are so oriented, but when you're asking about life as a whole, the temporal scope of your concern is unlimited. Thus, to ask such a question requires not only looking beyond the popular answers but also beyond ordinary values and interests. It is to be in a frame of mind in which these values are not then valuable and these interests are not then interesting.

As we saw when we first enunciated the sense of the absurd, it arises from a ghastly, global perspective, an awful look at life as a whole. It sees a vast expanse of time and space, piddling regions of which are occupied by brief bits called people. The problem is how to incorporate this view from afar to your own life within. It is a very general sort of problem.

Specific concerns can be dealt with specifically. If you are thrilled or excited enough about something to forget everything else, you have no problem at all. If you are hurt or have just been fired, you have a problem. But it's a specific problem. You may or may not know how to deal with it, but it is clear to you what counts as solving it. Your arm is healed; you have a new job.

In everyday circumstances, your consciousness operates against a wider, vaguer background. This background neither matters nor fails to matter. It is just there. Something in it may subsequently catch your attention or arouse your concern, but that just changes the focal point. Still there is a specific object of concern against an amorphous background.

When you are faced with a particular problem and you are facing it squarely, solving it seems in effect to be solving everything. "Your problems will be over," as the savings and loan commercial says. Your debt worries, anyway. The current problem seems the only one, until there arises a new one or an old one you had swept under the rug. Narrowness of focus is not limited to problems. Let's say you're about to go out with someone exciting, or to see your favorite superstars in action, or to get away from it all for two weeks. You're looking forward to the big moment when it all begins. The excitement of anticipation. Oops! You forgot that it will all soon be over and you'll be back where you began, albeit one gratification more to the good. But until you realize that fact, obvious as it is when you think of it, the thrill to come is what counts. Even if it will soon become the thrill that was.

The general problem of life has no particular solution. It concerns that amorphous background that's normally unquestioned. Is there any way to deal with it?

Transcending Transience

All things must pass. So, what else is new?

Indeed, all things must pass. This is nothing new. Realizing this is nothing new either. What is newer than this realization is a realization about it: if all things must pass, then among them is the realization that all things must pass. You can't spend all your time contemplating the fact that everything is transient.

Still, it might be suggested, anyone who realizes, if only from time to time, that all things must pass is affected in between by that realization. He may, for example, be chronically depressed, though only occasionally conscious of the reason for his depression. Or he may be cynical, contemptuous of others and himself alike for what they all have in common—the miserable destiny of doom lurking behind the delusively purposeful endeavors of everyday life. Or he may play the fool, seeing silliness as the only alternative to dreariness and defeatism. Whatever his attitude and his mood, surely it can be the product of his occasional conscious recognition of everything's fleetingness. He is living out that recognition in the way he sees others and in the way he acts in the presence of others.

If nothing has any ultimate significance, who said it should in the first place? Who are we to think that there must be a reason for our being here? Out of ignorance, primitives found a place for themselves in the cosmos. For us, even to try is out of arrogance.

We know that the question of life's meaning and our perception that it lacks an answer comes from taking a cosmic perspective. Looking at things as a whole we find nothing. Nothing but the things, that is. What did you expect? A prize for being here? A certificate of participation? Don't be silly.

Try to understand that the only way in which things can become meaningless is by your being in a frame of mind that renders them so. If you insist on things having a lasting value, if you insist on things adding up to something, if you insist that there is some ultimate tie-up, forget it. But why this insistence? Who needs unity, permanence, and ultimacy? "We do, that's who," you say; I say we don't. We only think we do as long as we retain the cosmic frame of mind that imposes these all-embracing demands in the first place.

So the source of our problem is the frame of mind in which we perceive there to be a problem. Should we therefore rid ourselves of this frame of mind? Should we make an attempt to return to our everyday follies? Can we do this in good conscience? Can we do it at all?

Surely our cosmic reflections cannot be forgotten, and should not if they are valid. That's assuming the respect due truth, even the truth that hurts. But this respect needn't become obsession. There is no reason why you should spend the rest of your life thinking to yourself, "I'm going to die. . . . Nothing matters. . . . It's all a joke. . . . I'm going to die. . . ." There are other things to think about.

Still, there is the nagging thought that these dreadful reflections, even when dormant, will permeate your life nonetheless. Maybe they do already and have done so for a long time. Maybe this book only reinforces them. It may be that these reflections, whenever they occur, are simply the conscious articulations of an endless mood perhaps of alternating benign depression and malignant despair. But then again, this chronic mood may be the long-term effect of these occasional reflections.

Well, there must be some way out. There must be some way to deal with the gruesome effect of looking at life through an unsparingly wide-angled lens. Forgetting doesn't seem to be the answer. True, the quest for the eternal, for what transcends transience, begins with the reflection that everyday experiences, however pleasant and delightful, cannot last. Forget their fleetingness and you forget the brevity and futility of life itself. But how to forget? You can't do it directly, for you might not remember to forget. Or you might, in trying to forget, be afraid that you will remember. This is something like the feeling you might have at the edge of a cliff. You're not afraid of slipping; you're not afraid that someone will push you—you're afraid you will jump! The very thought that you might makes you think that you will. Similarly, the thought that you can go on living without getting obsessed with how short and futile your life is may give rise to the thought that you won't be able to get rid of these thoughts. And the thought that you won't be able to get rid of them is enough to multiply them. (There is a certain lack of freedom in all this. It is the inability to cope with your lack of freedom. More on this in the last chapter.)

My approach to the problem is to follow its source to its logical conclusion. Let me show you what I mean. The problem is the recognition of life's brevity and of the transient experiences that make it up. The conclusion reached so far is that life, when and only when viewed as a whole, is futile and worthless and that the realization of this generates one or another of several chronic attitudes, none of which is chronically desirable. You can become obsessed with death, chronically bored, or permanently depressed. You can take the cynical and sarcastic approach. Or you can play "Let's Pretend" and treat it all as a vast joke or game. Whatever the tack you take, it would seem to be either alarmist or escapist. But maybe you can do better.

This all began with a reflection on the transience of experiences and therefore the transience of values. My response is: What did you expect? Of course you can't hold onto experiences. The best you can do is prolong them until they fade or falter. You can remember them from time to time, but memories fade also. The point is that experiences are essentially temporal. When they're finished happening, they're over. What can you do about that? Nothing. That's the way experiences are. What else could they be?

Thus, to seek the permanent and the eternal is in effect to try to hang onto the past. But the past, like the present and future, consists of experiences that can only pass. To seek the eternal is to try to escape time itself. The absurdity of this attempt lies in the fact that even if you were to live forever, you'd still be living in time. You could still be worried about the meaning of everything, about whether you really would never die, whether your suffering might someday be endless, and so on.

I have said that to hold onto experiences, as if you could, is to live in the past. Of course the thought that *all* your experiences will someday be past is probably what really bothers you. But why should that bother you now? It is as if your worry consists in thinking ahead to after your death and, once dead, having nothing but your life, which is now in the past, to look back upon. In any case, why look back upon it when it isn't even over yet?

Most important is the realization that now is forever. I don't mean that now lasts forever. The point is that you can never outlive the present. It always keeps up with you. I admit this is a triviality from the logical point of view, since *now,* by definition, is that moment contemporaneous with the reference to it. But it is still a triviality worth focusing on. There will never come the time when you can look back and say of life, "It's all over now." Life as a whole can never be looked back upon, because the moment of looking back is part of life, even if the last. Besides, the last moment of life can never be experienced as such. You may know you're about to die, but you cannot experience dying any more than you can experience falling asleep.

To live eternally is not to live endlessly. It is to live in the present. And that is all you can ever do. You can *think of* the past and the future, but you can only *be in* the present. You will never be anywhen else.

Alienation: Faulty Connections 2

It isn't easy trying to face up to life as a whole, but being conscious makes it hard not to. The feelings expressed in Chapter 1, and the attempt to deal with them, arose from a sense of isolation and separateness that will be described more fully in this chapter. There seemed to be no way to rationalize one's life in a world devoid of ultimate meaning, no way to bridge the gap between one's own smallness and the vastness of a pointless world. The solution given—living in the present—required a kind of calculated amnesia to stifle such dreary thoughts once and for all and to rub out the need for meaning. That solution is easier said than done, for what is to keep those thoughts and that need from returning? Distractions aren't effective enough. Perhaps there is a more positive and helpful answer.

The idea we will examine here is that a meaningful life can be achieved if a person is able to find something larger than himself to identify with, something whose meaning and value transcend the scope and duration of an individual life. Part of this idea is that meaningful personal relationships and meaningful involvement in activities of whatever sort require identification with the situation at hand.

Sounds like a pretty good idea, doesn't it? I wish I could agree. Instead, I'm going to spend the whole chapter trying to show that the only outcome of this effort at meaningful identification is alienation of one type or another. Such identification turns out to be an alluring pipe dream.

Since I define *alienation* in relation to identification, I want to make as clear as I can what I mean by *identification.* When a person identifies with something, he ascribes an essential connection between himself and it. He feels himself to be part of it, not just casually but in a special way. What makes this connection special is that he feels that the "object of identification" somehow represents him. If he identifies with a group, for example, he can feel pride in the group and, derivatively, in its members, just as if he were feeling pride in himself. Pride, after all, is an emotion that is ordinarily self-directed. Again, if the person identifies with a cause, then the feeling of importance he has about this cause is like a feeling of self-importance, not just in degree but in kind. Also, a person can identify with the particular situation he's in and the people he's with. His conception of himself, for the time being, is inseparable from his conception of the situation and the others.

Identification isn't automatic. Instead of a unity, the person may feel an opposition between himself and what he might, but doesn't, identify with. He might feel isolated from the group, undevoted to the cause, or separate from other people. He doesn't "relate." This lack of identification is one form of alienation we will discuss.

Alienation comes in many varieties, but there are two main types. Today it is common to speak of being, or feeling, alienated from something, be it your job, your family, your country, or even yourself (more on self-alienation in the next chapter). This type of alienation is a lack of identification with something you feel you ought to be able to identify with. I'll call it the alienation of *non*identification. There is also what I call the alienation of *mis*-identification, of falsely identifying with something. I'll explain this later on.

Nonidentification

This type of alienation may be specific to a particular situation or it may be general and pervasive. An example of the first may occur during a conversation with friends. Perhaps they're discussing something of no interest to you, like the stock market or auto racing. As a result, you feel entirely "out of it," or maybe downright disgusted. Whatever the case, you feel separate from the others, at least for the time being. After all, if the conversation turns to your favorite subject, say rock-and-roll music of the mid-fifties, your feeling of alienation quickly vanishes. For all you know, somebody else is now alienated.

Generalized alienation doesn't need a dull subject or a boring activity to generate it. No matter what is going on, you just can't get involved. Nothing catches your interest and produces excitement. It's not the people, either. You're not put off by them. It doesn't matter whom you're with, and your feeling isn't due to headache, worry, or momentary depression. You don't have "tired blood," or any other commercially popular complaint. Nothing in particular is the matter.

What is it, then? What keeps you from getting involved, from being motivated, from relating to others? Maybe your problem is that you think too much. Maybe it keeps occurring to you that everything going on will sooner or later come to an end, that the people around you will die, and that you yourself will die, too. Nothing can excite you because you immediately see beyond it to its conclusion. In a sense, it's over before it begins. Or, you look backward. You realize that you've done this, said this, or heard this a million times before. In short, nothing is fresh, curious, or appealing to you. Everything is old hat.

If this is how you feel, what can you think about other people who, so far as you can tell, naïvely accept the joys of life without question and whose idea of a big problem is a tax increase? On the one hand, you feel utter contempt for them, seeing how their consciousness is so restricted that they can enjoy themselves despite what there is to be realized about life. On the other hand, you feel a certain envy toward them. You wish you could turn your thinking off. If only you could just relax. Perhaps you wonder what they think of you. You probably think they consider you unfriendly, boring, depressing. Oh well, they can't be expected to understand.

Of course, it might occur to you that there are others who share your feelings—maybe even one of your group. He simply happens to be better than you at faking interest. Or did you suppose yourself to be the first ever to have such feelings? Don't be silly, thinking has been indulged in before. Your plight isn't unique.

In everyday life, this utter despair of relentless, mindless matter impinging endlessly on our puny lives tends to be suppressed. Life must go on, and for this purpose masks, screens, and habits help. People prefer boredom to agitation, repetition to revolution, rocking chairs to rocking boats. Conventions and conveniences, schedules and procedures keep things going, tell you what to do, make sense of what others do, and make life, if not easy, at least relatively clear-cut.

On rare occasions, there is some comfort in sharing your feelings with others, depressing as these feelings are. "Share and share alike," I always say. But part of the feeling being shared is one's essential aloneness. Despite sharing the feeling, there is still your having it as opposed to the other's having it, and that's part of the feeling. It includes the sense that whatever is going on will ultimately amount to nothing. Your feeling of alienation from others and their activities, felt even during your feigned participation (especially), has a counterpart in your view of those who don't seem alienated. As you observe others engaged in their affairs, the observation is clogged with the thought that all is for nought, that they are but puppets, unaware of the strings yet to be cut. You recognize in even the most purposeful and resolute actions their utter futility. You note to yourself that motivations can operate only within the confines of one's blindness to his ultimate fate.

Take a poignant example. A comedian gets up in front of an audience with one purpose in mind: to get laughs. He'll get them all right, mostly out of politeness no doubt, but what a pitiful reward. Implicitly he is saying to them, "I am here to say funny things that will make you laugh. So laugh." They are there to hear funny things and to laugh. What a harmonious relationship; what a marvelous arrangement! Hundreds of people who don't know each other getting together to hear things that will make them laugh and enable them to hear others laugh, even though they'll go home later little different from before.

Or, suppose the jokes aren't funny. An uncomfortable feeling develops, not only in the performer but in the audience, who feels sorry for him and maybe forces out a few lame laughs to make him feel good. Maybe they boo and hiss, resenting the fact that they spent time and money for this. The comedian tries harder, but it only gets worse; he's a total flop. Or perhaps his act does go over. He has them in stitches. They're laughing to the point of agony. He won't let up. Their tears are flooding the arena. "You're too funny. Please stop," they pray. Finally he does.

The very idea of performance—whether comic, dramatic, athletic; as a clerk, a waiter, a teacher, or a doctor—involves a person on display. This seems to produce either humiliation or, if that is recognized, alienation. Particularly when the performance is prefabricated, we have a case of one person doing something calculated to produce a desired effect in an audience. What degradation, what stooping! But people do it every day, formally and informally, professionally and as amateurs—producing effects, creating impressions, conveying ideas.

Who deserves greater sympathy, the performer or the audience, the one who is humiliated or the one who is the unwitting witness to the humiliation? The performer's lack of recognition is itself a humiliation. As long as the audience and the performer remain blind to, or suppress, the realization that all is for nought, that the greatest of goals and the noblest of purposes wither and die into nothing, then everyday life can go on, its antics pretending to meanings that have no business being there.

Enough of this tirade. I was describing the alienation of nonidentification and illustrating how it can occur in particular contexts or be a pervasive experience. Perhaps I should mention further examples of alienation in particular contexts, since the generalized variety usually develops from concrete situations. Most common, I imagine, is alienation from one's work. After all, if you have a job, you probably spend a major portion of your time doing it. You have a right to expect to be able to identify with it. You want to be able to feel that what is going on is your doing, at least partly, and that the effects are beneficial to yourself or to what you believe in. You don't want to feel used or exploited. But how many jobs don't yield alienation sooner or later?

Institutions are often responsible for alienation. A person expects the government or any other institution affecting his life to reflect his interests. He expects public officials to represent his interests, at least to the extent compatible with the interests of others. He expects to participate, directly or indirectly, in the decision-making processes that bear upon him. But all these expectations are not easily fulfilled in today's world. Many people, brought up in the virtues of patriotism and related sentiments, have been disillusioned to the point of wondering whether the country they live in is really their own. This is alienation.

Separateness from Others

Alienation from institutions and from impersonal goings on might be tolerable if relationships with other people were fulfilling. Yet there is a sense of ultimate aloneness that cannot be diverted forever. Even love, which conquers all, cannot hide the threat of separation. Let's save love for later in this section and first look at other relationships.

We probably have to admit that many of our relations with others occur at barely a conscious level. It is hard to pay particular attention to people we see in such everyday places as supermarkets, offices, highways, and theaters. Even if you think of yourself as humane and compassionate, most of the time, most people are of no concern to you, for you are not even conscious of them. It's not a question of limited feeling but of limited span of consciousness. Until I brought up the subject, how many of the people you care about were you thinking of at this moment?

In everyday situations, if I attempt to raise my level of attention to people to a conscious one, I must either conceal the effort or run the risk of being regarded as nosy, pushy, or phony. The fact is that most people like to (or are afraid not to) follow the path of least resistance, the way of clichéd routines, in their daily affairs. Being personal ("You're beautiful") or unpredictable (bidding an unexpected "goodbye") is often a shock. Easier is the use of stereotyped devices such as "How are you?" "Nice day today," and "I'll have to be going now."

Now you might feel grateful for social conventions that prescribe moves for all sorts of situations. Interacting with people you don't know is not easy, after all, precisely because you don't know each other. The unwritten code book provides convenient ways of filling time in the social situations that crop up during the day. Besides, you can't get personal with everyone, but what about your friends and those others you frequently see? Of course, any relation of one person to another is always partial. However much you may share interests, feelings, and thoughts, there is inevitably a surplus of each person that is not shared. All communication is partial, however complete the rapport. Indeed, a person doesn't even notice much of what he himself thinks and feels. Figuratively speaking, then, people can overlap but never coincide.

Suppose you are with another person. To the extent that you reflect about the situation, you are bound to question your own interest in the other person and in what is going on. Equally, you may question the other's interest in you and in the situation. You may even wonder about the other's doubts about you and about his wondering about your doubts about him. This sort of doubting and wondering can occur, since it entails reflection about the situation, only if the intensity of talk or activity is not too great. Involvement yields intensity, but hesitation limits involvement. Also, such doubting and wondering is possible only for someone capable of serious reflection. Apparently, most people aren't capable of it most of the time. For them, routine transactions will do. And even when people become relatively open and intimate, still there is a residue of secrecy. There is always something to hide.

Now one of the things about consciousness is that it can't be consciously turned off. Once you're aware of something, you can't just decide not to be aware of it any longer. That would require the impossible achievement of being aware of being aware and deciding that being aware is not what you want to be. What is needed and what is usually available is not decision but distraction. Things, events, duties, and people provide it. They catch your attention and prevent you from continuing to be aware of what you were aware of. Even when you're aware of being aware of the situation, distractions inadvertently inhibit your reflection and squelch your doubts. In short, they make it easy to limit reflexive awareness. Of course, the blessings of companionship are not without the burdens of devotion. And when this burden is, for example, having to listen to an interminable story, moments of reflection recur, perhaps yielding feelings of separateness. The other person may appear an alien thing that produces words, displays feeling, and expects response. You may remind yourself that the other is a person but still a distinct, separate one. Whatever the other says or does, there is always more to him than those things, or maybe there isn't.

There is a positive side to all this. When we filter out all the individual differences, the things we like or admire in others and the things we don't, there remains one thing that can tie people together—the very thing, paradoxically, that keeps people forever apart. Insofar as we are aware of others as being the same sort as ourselves—conscious beings aware of being conscious —we feel a closeness to them, particularly when we recognize the relative irrelevance of the qualities that distinguish us one from another. As a conscious being aware of my own finitude and helplessness in the face of time, I am aware of others as being the same as I. My sense of smallness gives way to a compassion for others, who are no bigger or smaller than I. And then I can't feel sorry for myself so easily.

This general empathy is not wholly good, I must admit. To experience it, one must abstract from the individual differences between people and generalize from any particulars that one knows. For this feeling to apply to everyone, familiar and unfamiliar, past, present, and future, one must be alienated from any concrete situation that one is in. How can you engage in a conversation, play a game, or demonstrate for peace while maintaining a generalized feeling of empathy that applies to all people, both good and evil and in between? How can what is happening right now be meaningful and involving when dwarfed by such a totalistic feeling? How can you love anyone or care for anyone in particular, your friends or those who need help, when the feeling felt is so awfully universal? You can't.

So, what ultimately ties you to everyone also separates you from anyone in particular. United with everyone by the bond of consciousness, you are at the same time barred from everyone by the gulf of consciousness. You are alone. Even if you bring up the subject of the preceding paragraphs, this strange feeling of general empathy and the alienation that goes with it, in an attempt to share it with someone else, no sooner do you sense this feeling in the other's reverent expression than you begin to wonder whether what he feels is really the same as what you feel. You might even think, "How could *he* feel what *I* feel?" No sooner said than undone.

Perhaps you harbor no such doubts. You and the person you're with really do share this feeling of empathy, complete with a smile of comprehension and a tear of sorrow. But what do you do? What can you say? Any concrete option seems puny and pathetic; even discussing this feeling seems useless. You have the choice between paralysis and going on, anyway. Or is there a choice? Not really. You feel paralyzed, but it wears off and you go on, anyway. You share this feeling with your friend; the two of you meditate on it briefly, and then it's back to work or whatever. The coffee break is over.

If there is any relationship that can transcend the alienating power of consciousness, surely it must be love. Mutual love, in which each feels an unconditional affection, respect, and concern for the other, comes closest to overcoming the feeling of aloneness. Sometimes love is described as the merging of two into one, and certainly it can feel that way. But how long will it last? Sooner or later, a person in love must raise this question, not because he wants to but because he can't help it. The question just comes up.

Love makes a person forget his troubles, his responsibilities, the miseries pervading the world. Love makes one oblivious to the future, at least for a while. It may make him forget himself. The trouble is that these side-effects don't last forever. The emotional peak that love attains eventually levels off, and the rest of reality rears its head. Then it's down to earth. Thinking returns. With or without any concrete reason, you may wonder how long the love will last; will the other change too much; will you yourself change? What if something happens to the other? The terror of doubt and uncertainty needs no special impetus. Maybe it's the fear of boredom or a sense of the absurdity of love: what makes that person so special? It's a dangerous question. Love is the answer only when there is no question. Questioning, and the self-reflection it entails, brings back that feeling of aloneness.

Misidentification

I hope the preceding examples illustrate the extent to which identification with something can fail. All it takes is the spontaneous realization of your separateness from whatever it is you're trying to identify with. This realization needn't be incessant. For some, it may occur rarely if ever. You may succeed in identifying with something, something other than yourself. That's what I call the alienation of misidentification.

Before explaining what I mean by misidentification, I should explain the reason for calling it *alienation.* An old legalistic (and philosophic) usage of *alienate* is to transfer or convey. Misidentification, then, means selling out, that is, trading what you are for what you're not. Unlike the alienation of nonidentification, the alienation of misidentification need not be conscious or felt. Indeed, when it is conscious, as we will see, it is likely to yield to the alienation of nonidentification.

By *misidentification* I don't mean simply having mistaken opinions about yourself. No doubt everyone thinks certain distorted things about himself, and no doubt there are certain things about himself that he doesn't think. What I am talking about is mistaken identification with something. People identify with other persons, with groups, with causes, with professions, with principles, and even with the entire universe. To identify with something doesn't mean to think you are the same thing as it, not literally anyway. If I identify with philosophy, for example, I don't think that I *am* philosophy. True, identification can involve ascribing literal identity, as when Hitler said, "I am Germany." He didn't merely identify himself *with* the fatherland—he identified himself *as* the fatherland. Normally, though, the identity is only metaphorical. I don't believe I am literally philosophy, but perhaps I feel a part of it and identify my interests with its interests. What's good for me is good for it, and vice versa.

Sometimes identification with something includes a personification of the object. That's how a captain sees his ship and how a loyal citizen sees his country (in both cases as a "she"). With or without personification, this identification includes the phenomenon of ordinarily self-directed emotions felt toward the object of identification. Such emotions are pride (or honor, or dignity) and shame (or disgrace, or humiliation). Normally, a person is proud or ashamed of himself. Of someone else he feels admiration or contempt. But when there is identification, these other-directed feelings are replaced by self-directed ones. An obvious example is a parent's feelings about his child, whom he regards as an extension of himself, whose actions "reflect" on him, who "carries my name." I might mention that names, which are symbols of both the identifier and the object of identification, help mediate the process, uniting the identifier and the object. For example, to think of yourself as an American is in effect to identify with America.

Patriotism is a classic example of identification in the metaphorical style. Patriots are proud of their country (and its flag, also symbolic of the country), unless it (they) happens to suffer from "national disgrace." An attack on their country is an attack on them, and it must be defended at all costs. Those able to fight for its (their) honor must be willing to make the ultimate sacrifice in the cause of its (their) defense. Plainly, patriotism is a socially reinforced type of identification. More on such reinforcement in the next section.

The feeling of oneness that some people claim to have with the universe is another illustration of metaphorical identification. Such people may regard each thing as nothing more than a manifestation of the universal Self. There is no genuine division in the world, they think, no real conflict but only the illusion of it. This identification is not only the identification of part with whole but of part with part. Everything and everyone have a mystical identity with each other since each is a manifestation of the whole.

On a smaller scale, in a group of people, there is a felt identity not only with the group but between the members (as brothers, teammates, or children of God). Identification with the whole (as in *"Deutschland über alles'*) thus generates identification with the parts: *"E pluribus unum."*

The felt connection here among persons is not itself personal. Rather, it is mediated by the whole that each person belongs to or is a part of. It can be politically useful to connect people via their respective connections to the whole, that abstraction with which they mutually identify. "Ask not what your country can do for you; ask what you can do for your country." I refer to the whole as an abstraction because countries, for example, are not conscious entities that have the capacity for joy and sorrow, with interests independent of those of its citizens. And yet countries and other institutions are treated as if they were sentient things in their own right. Patriotism and other types of loyalty (for example, corporate) are directed at these abstractions, rather than to the people who compose them. And where there is identification with the achievements of particular members, such as with American athletes or Russian cosmonauts, it is focused on what they represent (America or Russia), not on who they are individually.

Sometimes the members' mutual identification with each other and with the group is the product of their treatment by another group. Obvious examples include racial, sexual, and economic oppression. In each case, the mutual identification of the members of the oppressed class stems from their conscious recognition of their oppression as a class. To overcome this oppression, perhaps it is necessary for them to adopt in a positive form the very identification (for example, as black or as female) by which they are distinguished for oppression. The quality that previously disgraced them becomes the quality that enhances them.

Despite its psychological advantages, especially in the case just mentioned, all identification is mistaken. Whether it's with your town, your team, or your temple, identification with anything but yourself is mistaken. You have no business whatsoever being proud of the achievements of anyone else, in being ashamed of anyone else's failures. You are you and they are they. You can admire them or, if you insist, despise them for what they are or do. But the identity between you and them, like the identity between you and what you belong to, is fantasy. Admittedly, I called it metaphorical, but as long as you feel pride or shame —emotions that belong only to you—the identification might as well be literal.

Such identification is mistaken insofar as it generates emotions that are inappropriate. In other words, these emotions are vicarious. They are prompted by actions and experiences that are not your own and you respond as if they were your own. This "as if" is provided by identification. Identifying with a group is a psychologically appealing act that has no logical basis. Pride in the deeds of others is vicarious, shame gratuitous. To be sure, the alienation of misidentification may be gratifying. I never denied that. People who are proud of their leaders and heroes, their culture and traditions, perhaps need something bigger and better than themselves to be proud of. Still, the collective is a collection of individuals. People can care for each other and share with each other, but nobody can be represented by anybody but himself.

In denouncing identification and in associating love and mysticism with it, I am not objecting to them but only to a certain way of describing them.

Love is sometimes thought of as a relation of oneness with another, and mysticism as a similar relation with the universe. Now, if they really were "relations of oneness," then indeed they would be cases, however blissful, of misidentification in the way just explained. I want to suggest an alternative description, one that accounts for why the first way of describing these experiences (as relations of oneness) is so plausible.

From my own experience and from others' reports, it seems that these heightened moments of seeming relatedness with another or with the universe involve what is sometimes labeled *ego loss*. A person loses the sense of himself as separate and feels a sense of merging instead; thus the appealing term *oneness*. I would prefer to describe these experiences as the result of losing self-consciousness. These blissful moments are essentially unreflexive. In such a state, you can't say, "*I* have lost my sense of self."

Afterwards, it is perfectly natural to describe the experience in this way. Later, in the state of reflecting upon that egoless (unreflexive) state, you recall not feeling separate (from the other or from the world as a whole). It is appealing to describe the situation as one of unity. Rather, the experience was lacking in the usual sense of disunity, of separateness, that results from self-consciousness.

Alien Values

Let's digress (ever so slightly) to the subject of what I call *alien values*. By these I mean values that a person accepts as his own even though they're not. They may or may not be genuine values (that's why I don't call them *false values*). What makes them alien is how they are accepted. The most common example is of something that people accept because, each person thinks, people accept it. Social habits such as smoking and drinking, religion and wearing neckties, are done (or not done) because "everybody" does them. In different cases the referent of "everybody" varies—it depends on the group a person refers to in making his decisions. Much hackneyed social psychology might be mentioned here, for example, the talk about peer groups, status, and social acceptance; but, suffice it to say that each person in a group acts in reference to the group as a whole, that is, to everybody else. Everybody subordinates himself to everybody else.

Interesting psychological and philosophical points can be made about this phenomenon. I suspect my next book will deal with this sort of thing. For now, it is enough to say that each subordinates himself to the group and that it is the reference to the group, the idea of group acceptance, that legitimizes the group's values for each member. "If everybody accepts it, it must be good. Ten million Elks can't be wrong." Furthermore, as a rule, members of a group who reject or even question the group's values are ostracized or pronounced insane or subversive.

Particularly important are the groups you are born into, such as family, religion, and country. They and the values they embody seem to admit of no alternatives. As a child surrounded by adults who support country and religion as sacrosanct, who are you to think any differently? Nobody, that's who. You're aware that there are awful people around like commies and atheists but you would never be one of them. Even when you reach adulthood, itself a socially defined category, and begin to question some of the basic values that "everyone" accepts, outright rejection of these values is possible only with a lot of courage or a little company. Most people, it seems, never seriously question, let alone reject, the values of groups they're born into. Those who do are regarded as "going through a phase," as engaging in "typical teenage shenanigans," or, if they don't "get over it," as belonging to a "lunatic fringe." Thus, the socially accepted system of values is equipped to deal with those who don't accept it.

The result is that most people accept social values as real, natural, universal, and unconditional. They may even be unaware that alternatives are possible, let alone plausible. In this case, they cannot be aware of their beliefs as beliefs, for they accept their values as unopposable realities, not as options with alternatives. Thus, there is no obstacle to accepting these social values as their own.

The social acceptance and resultant entrenchment of values do not occur in a vacuum. The routine and ritual of everyday life that maintain the legitimacy of these values by making them seem objective. Certain styles of clothes are worn; different styles signal different roles and positions in society. Different roles and positions signify different degrees of social importance. Again, there are certain ways in which "things are done." Except for those things that are not permitted at all, "there's a time and place for everything." More examples of routines and social forms:

Eat three meals a day.

What do you do? For a living, I mean.

Time to get up. You're wasting your life away.

How are the Mets doing? Lost again.

Nice day today.

Everybody's against war, but . . .

Where are you from? Oh, I passed through there once.

I'd like you to meet . . .

We met here last year.

It's a pleasure to meet you.

The very existence of something may give it significance. A number of people doing it substantiate its significance: going to church, trying to lose weight. Mass media provide the ultimate sanction. If it's on the news, it must be terribly important. Often, what's happening is not the news but people seeing or hearing the news of what's happening. Anything unreported isn't worth considering and might as well not be happening.

The Dilemma of Alienation

The two types of alienation, nonidentification and misidentification, constitute a dilemma. One leads to the other, the other leads back to the first, and both are unsatisfactory. The dilemma is really with identification itself. You identify with something until you realize that it isn't you, that you have been falsely identifying. People have this experience with family, college, and country. Having recognized the falsity of your identification, you thereby can no longer continue with it and come to feel alienated from whatever you previously identified with. At this point, either you realize you're on your own, or you look for something else to identify with, say the "Movement." You haven't figured out that identification is false in principle, no matter what you identify with. And then, for one reason or another (for example, boredom or disillusionment), you lose this identification and feel alienated again. The process can go on and on until you settle into some permanent identification (for example, with middle America), or until it dawns on you that identification with something other than yourself is fundamentally mistaken. Even when you realize that, the process may still continue, to the extent that you are subject to pressures from others. There will always be people around you rooting for the home team, supporting their President, or backing the union. You will be forced into either identifying (or pretending to) or being alienated from those around you.

I want to make it clear that I am not advocating personal separatism. The dilemma of alienation does not mean you shouldn't relate to other people and support worthy causes. It's identification I'm objecting to, treating as your own what isn't. I'm advocating personal integrity, not separatism. As long as you insist on identifying with things, you'll be stuck in the dilemma of identification. First you'll resort to one kind of false identification or another, until you wake up to the fact that it's delusional. Then you'll suffer from the conscious type of alienation, that of nonidentification. You may feel the need to find something else to identify with. For this purpose, there are plenty of established organizations and countless offbeat cults available. (Consult your local directory.)

The only way out of this dilemma is to recognize that you can't identify or define yourself in external terms. That is, you can't conceive of what you are as what you're not without being grossly mistaken. In the next two chapters, we'll look at the problem of self-definition. First, we'll examine what it means to feel at home with yourself, and then we'll investigate the unpleasant alternative of self-alienation. Finally, we'll look at what is involved in having a self-conception, an identity.

Self-Alienation: Cutting and Splicing 3

Before taking a positive look at self-images (in the next chapter), I want to examine what you might call the "fractured self," despite the fact that there is no single good description of the whole range of phenomena that fall under the heading of *self-alienation.*

I'm maintaining my double use of the term *alienation* to include both nonidentification and misidentification. We'll examine cases in which a person fails to identify with part of what he is. It may be his body or physical features, or it may be his actions that seem somehow not to be his own. Sometimes it is difficult to identify with what you are for others, whether it is how you look or how you express yourself. Or it may be your reputation that you can't identify with, not that you should. Finally, you may fail to identify with part of what you are for yourself, your own feelings, for example.

Misidentification about yourself can occur in various ways. I don't mean merely being mistaken about yourself, as surely everyone is to some extent. Rather, I mean over- or underidentifying with what you are. You may emphasize one aspect of yourself to the exclusion of others, thinking that this is all that you are and discounting the rest. An important instance is identifying excessively with what you are for others. Equally important is limiting your identification to what you are for yourself.

Going through the Motions

The scientific way of making sense of the world doesn't provide you with anything personal. As mentioned in Chapter 1, science may underscore the lack of meaningful relation between you and the world. Moreover, despite its pretensions to being comprehensive, science leaves the world in fragments, at least

36

as far as your or my consciousness is concerned. Scientific laws may cover everything, but they don't unify the phenomena they connect. Maybe that's an exaggeration. What I should say, I guess, is that they don't unify things in a humanly relevant way. Scientific laws find no purpose in the scheme of things. They present a scheme without a schemer.

Human actions have a kind of unity that natural phenomena viewed scientifically seem to lack. Human actions are united by purposes, that is, the intents of the actors. Whenever you do something, what you're doing has a beginning, a middle, and an end. Generally, an action is begun with a certain end in mind, even if that end is not consciously recognized. (Here, *end* means both goal and finish.) If you meet with failure along the way, at least you know what you haven't done. Where intention is present, there is success or failure. A sense of purpose unifies the series of events that make up the action.

Human actions begin and end. Natural occurrences start and stop. There's a difference there. Sure, we can talk about biological evolution, for example, as if the development of progressively higher forms of life reflected something somebody had in mind at the outset, but natural selection depends on unintended mutations, among other things. In general, the patterns science finds in events don't seem to need a designer. Even human history, a vast mixture of human actions and natural events, exhibits no purpose but to those who insist on imagining one. Only specific human actions really have intentions behind them and thus begin and end instead of merely starting and stopping.

The reason I mention all this is that it helps explain a basic type of self-alienation or dissociation. Have you ever experienced your own actions as if they lacked purpose, as if *you* weren't really performing them? Things done out of force of habit, such as shifting gears in a car, can easily be experienced this way. You're just going through the motions. Something is happening, but you don't have the feeling of doing it (not that anyone else is doing it). You may be daydreaming when suddenly you catch yourself in the act of doing something, almost as though you were observing someone else. Or, have you ever watched somebody else in action when you didn't know what he was doing? A good example is seeing someone talking in a phone booth. His moving lips might strike you as absurd, as would your own if you were making faces at yourself in the mirror. Each moment of motion seems unconnected with the rest; the series is fragmented. Silent movies are particularly good examples of this fragmentation. By distracting and detracting from purpose, silence and jerkiness enhance the portrayal of the ludicrous and the pathetic, as Charlie Chaplin so adroitly showed.

Sometimes I have a dissociated experience while writing this book. As I work at the typewriter, sometimes it seems as if these letters just land on the page automatically. Sometimes, in fact, right now, I watch my fingers punching various letters on the keyboard and I am amazed that these sentences are the result. Or, I reread something I've written and I wonder if it is I who wrote it. Sometimes you may experience your body and your actions as if they were those of a puppet. At least you are the puppeteer (unless you feel that someone else is pulling the strings). When you speak, it's as if you were your own ventriloquist.

These are examples of dissociation from your body (or parts of it) and from your actions. Your actions can be experienced as natural phenomena, mechanical rather than autonomous and purposive. Your body may seem to be the machine producing these events, your limbs the moving parts. They are perceived not as your own but outside yourself. Your actions are observed, not performed.

The separateness and fragmentation of one's actions go together. Actions seem separate from oneself because they lack the purpose involved in actions that are genuinely one's own. And lacking purpose, they lack the overarching meaning that would tie their parts together. Thus, they are internally disconnected as well as seeming disconnected from oneself. What is the cause of this type of self-alienation? Habits and routines may be to blame, since they don't require much attention or invention. Moreover, such dissociation can cause you to see your own actions as utterly pointless. Sometimes you see too far. When you cross the finish line the race is over, so what's the point of running it? You can't answer that, and yet you run it anyway. Then you wonder why you're running and maybe even whether it is you who's doing it. Thus, a sense of the absurd may generate dissociation from one's actions. (Chapter 1 noted conscious strategies that yield the same effect, such as acting absurdly on purpose or alienating yourself from the world by trying to do nothing.)

Most people, so it seems, are involved in most of the things they do. Actually, I suspect that behind the mask of involvement is more alienation than ordinarily imagined. Who knows how much human activity and interaction is pretended involvement? At any rate, where there *is* genuine involvement, the horizon of awareness stops at the prospective end of the present activity. This activity may be short- or long-term; it may consist of many subsequent steps leading to some relatively ultimate end. In either case, an activity constitutes a little world of its own, much

as does a drama or a symphony. It represents a total unit. Everything within it forms part of the whole, including even the obstacles. The whole is defined by the ruling purpose, and things
going on within are perceived as either helping or hindering.
During the course of action, everything irrelevant to the action
is more or less unperceived, although this can be changed in a
moment by the intrusion of a violent distraction or a disaster. If
you're taking an exam, making love, mopping the floor, or painting a picture, presumably you're conscious of what you're doing,
unless your mind is wandering. At that moment, everything else
in the world is irrelevant, including the future. However, your
attention would be quickly diverted by a fire, an explosion, or the
memory of a traumatic experience.

Normally, then, what you are doing, your present activity, is the
frame of reference for your consciousness. If you are acting
purposefully, then your thoughts will likely not extend beyond
that purpose. But when you can't focus on what you're doing (I
don't mean just a little daydreaming), and particularly when you
think too far into the future, your actions tend to lose their integrity—they either fall apart or feel alien or both. This is when
people sometimes feel that their only authentic gesture is to do
absolutely nothing. Thus, without a sense of purpose and involvement, a person can feel separato from his own actions. His
actions seem fragmented, lacking the connecting thread of purpose.

Another type of experience of fragmentation and self-dissocia-
tion is tied not to particular actions but to your life as a whole.
There are different aspects of your life that you relate to in different ways and that can't be combined satisfactorily. An obvious
example is the distinction between work and play. For most
people, work is intrinsically painful but necessary, while play is
fun but useless ("I must get back to work"; "Thank goodness it's
Friday"). This attitude may be due to the nature of the job or to
one's upbringing. Either way, it yields a bifurcated life, in which
one part is subordinated to the other. Similarly, different realms
of experience may seem to have no connection with one another; for example, the intellectual, the aesthetic, the political,
and the physical may seem worlds apart. To the extent that a
person identifies with one aspect of his life to the exclusion of
all others, his life lacks harmony and balance. He may resent the
time spent doing things irrelevant to the only activity he thinks
important. Equally, he may resent people who don't share his
restricted approach to life.

Fragmentation may be so severe that a person fails to identify
with even one particular aspect of his life. He feels like Humpty

Dumpty and has no hope of putting the pieces together again. His condition may be aggravated by social demands and bureaucratic nightmares to the point where he loses all sense of purpose in everything he hasn't given up trying to do. Not only is his life a shambles, he wonders whether it's really his own.

Being an Appearance

A second type of self-alienation requires another person to be aware of you. This is commonly called *self-consciousness*. Suppose you walk into a room full of people listening to a lecture. As you enter, their eyes turn toward you. You're acutely aware of their being aware of you. In fact, that is all you're aware of. You have a horrible sense of petrification. You feel like an object, a thing in their world. You are outside of yourself; you are there for them. Sometimes this feeling occurs when you think you're alone and then realize you're not—someone has quietly entered the room. The disclosure of another's presence sends a shudder of terror down your spine, even though there is no real danger. You might feel naked though fully clothed. Another case is when you make a fool of yourself or when the once hidden truth about yourself (you're a bastard, you're impotent) is revealed. Now they know. Now you're found out.

What counts here isn't so much what the other knows as his way of knowing it, namely by your unwitting exposure of yourself. That's what causes the embarrassment, that helpless feeling of subjugation to another's consciousness.

Alienation from how you appear to others may take a more chronic form. For example, if you are deformed or just plain ugly (by conventional standards), the presence of others may make you ashamed of yourself. You can either allow that shame to be a regular thing, or you can try to get rid of it. But if you are not to avoid others altogether, what can you do? You can pretend that they don't really see *you,* that what they do see isn't really you, but only your body. However, this requires effecting a mental separation of yourself from your body. Alienation from part of what you are (for others) is the price you must pay to avoid feeling embarrassment. You may try to compensate in some other way ("You'll like my personality!"), but by trying to escape what you are for others, by regarding your body as a shell, you are shielding yourself from them. "They're disgusted with my body, but not with me, for they're not even aware of me." It seems the only alternative is being disgusted with yourself.

Ideally, of course, it would be nice if people didn't take much account of bodily blemishes. Unfortunately, most people don't know you at all, let alone know you well, and thus can't be expected to know you "for yourself." And you can't (and shouldn't) avoid people forever. So you try either to blot out their consciousness of you, or to alienate from yourself what they are conscious of.

There are many ways to feel oppressed by others' consciousness of you. You may feel spied on. You may feel embarrassed by your bad breath or body odor. You may feel hurt at having a bad reputation for doing what you personally believe in. Whatever the case, it seems the pain you feel is predicated on an overemphasis of what you are for others. I'm not saying that what you are for others doesn't count at all. The question is how much it should count. It takes courage not to let it count for too much.

Some people have so little integrity or autonomy that they think of themselves exclusively in terms of what they are for others. A beautiful woman may be just as proud of her looks as a homely one is ashamed of hers, but while the homely one may try to disidentify with her looks (or vainly try to make herself up) and compensate with her personality, the beautiful one over-identifies with her looks, thinking of herself primarily, if not exclusively, as a beautiful woman. No doubt the fact that everybody else sees her that way can only reinforce this overidentification and make it extremely difficult for her to be anything else in the eyes of others, however hard she tries.

Overidentification with what you are for others needn't be painful or pathological if you happen to enjoy it. Still, it leaves something to be desired, as many beauties, politicians, and actors eventually realize. It becomes pathological when it dawns on the person that he really isn't anything else but what he is for others. And this realization makes him see that of course he is something else—what he is for himself. Politicians and entertainers who suffer from this problem of a public "image" often try to solve it by distinguishing between their private and their public lives, but this is just another form of self-alienation.

There are other examples of overidentification with one's exterior. The most extreme is the case of the exhibitionist. I don't feel qualified to venture into the psychological ramifications of this type, but a few generalizations won't hurt. Presumably, the exhibitionist desperately needs attention, and it doesn't particularly matter from whom. He feels so unsure of himself and his significance that anybody will do. And yet by exhibiting himself (or otherwise showing off), he is not relating to the other in anything approaching an intimate manner. He's just presenting an appearance. But for him to get the kind of gratification he needs, basking in the glow of attention, he must identify fully with that appearance. And so he does.

In this section, we've seen a variety of cases of self-alienation involving over- or underidentification with one's outer appearance. One feels either overly attached to it (or stuck with it), or else severely detached from it. The person may be more or less conscious of what he's doing, depending on the circumstances. Now let's turn to the case in which the person is explicitly conscious of the relation between himself and the appearance he presents. There are actually two cases here, one in which he manipulates his appearance and the other in which his appearance seems to manipulate him.

Faking It

Everybody is a fake, at least some of the time. If not by commission, then by omission. What we reveal isn't necessarily what we feel, and much of what we feel we don't reveal. This is partly due to the limitations on communication in routine situations, so deeply engrained in us are everyday roles and gestures. Here, the lack of communication is relatively unconscious. I want to focus on the conscious variety, whether it is positive deception or simply holding back. In particular, I want to look at what deception does to the deceiver.

As we've already seen, people often fear becoming an object to another. They fear exposure, manipulation, and derision. By deceiving another person, you may be trying to avoid these fearful consequences, indeed by subjecting the other person to them instead. Obviously, deception can serve the purpose of achieving your own ends at the other's expense. Whatever your reason, part of what you're doing in manipulating the situation is presenting an appearance that isn't you to the other person. You want him to think that it is you. Of course, in trying to hide from him, you may be subject to the fear of being found out. Needless to say, that fear can justify itself, since it may cause your deception to fail.

To try to escape from another requires a kind of escape from yourself. I don't mean this moralistically, but rather that putting on an act requires behaving in a way that isn't expressive of yourself but of whom you want the other to think you are. You're separating yourself from your actions. It's not like stage acting, although that can be schizoid sometimes. On the stage you're not actually trying to fool anybody. In a play, an actor tries to be convincing; in real life, an actor tries to convince. There is a difference.

Refusing to express yourself and instead expressing a fake self is one phenomenon. Another is simply being unable to express yourself. Take any occasion in which the "rules of the game" require certain sorts of behavior and presume certain sorts of underlying feelings. The scene may be a street corner, an office, a ballpark, a mortuary, or a university. Behaving yourself, in an effort to avoid offending others or to avoid involving them, may interfere with being yourself. No doubt there are those who don't recognize this, who feel at home in every situation whatever its dictates. They behave themselves and think they're being themselves. But once you recognize the limitations, the arbitrariness, the impersonality, and the prefabrication typifying everyday situations, you're faced with the problem of how to act. You're no longer content merely to react. I'm not saying that you should, in every case, make yourself offensive or otherwise obtrusive. Maybe you shouldn't. However, no matter what your action, you're aware of a conflict between expressing yourself and doing what you're expected (presumably) to do. And to avoid alienating yourself from the other, you must alienate yourself from yourself.

An added point about these situations: sometimes both (or all) persons involved may feel the same way, that is, hemmed in by the rules. But neither recognizes that the other feels the same way, and each acts as if the other doesn't. If only they both knew —but they don't. Rather than take a risk, they behave themselves in deference to the imagined wishes of the other. And what are the rules they're both following? Nothing more than a general, mutual expectation that certain things are to be done in certain situations. As a result of knowing the rules, two people can mutually misrepresent themselves by misconstruing the other.

This phenomenon can occur even when the rule applies only to the two persons involved. In a marriage, for example, a couple can come to develop certain mutual expectations as the result of what you might call "uncontested precedents." These determine who washes the dishes, who takes out the garbage, and when and how love is made. A status quo becomes established, and neither person sees fit to challenge it for fear of antagonizing the other. Little by little, they both begin to feel constricted by the relationship. Neither feels free to be himself, and neither realizes the other feels the same way. Only open communication can solve the problem, but that may be one of the things their unspoken rules prohibit.

In both the above cases, each person is self-alienated in order (he thinks) not to be alienated from the equally self-alienated other.

All of the examples in this section illustrate the type of self-alienation due to limited self-expression. It depends essentially on the presence of another, for the conflict is between how the person sees himself and how the other sees him (more precisely, how he imagines the other to see him). He may create a false self intentionally, in order to manipulate the other. Or, due to the limitations of the situation and his own unwillingness to break the rules, he may be unable to express himself genuinely.

I won't pass moral judgment on the self-alienation of faking it. Even when the deception is deliberate, it may be justified (you don't want to hurt others; you do need that job). As for socially sanctioned deception, such as most common courtesies, I recognize the ideal of total communication, but I find it difficult to envisage the utopia in which everybody cares about everyone else and wants everyone else to care about him, and in which there is universal trust. Short of such a utopia, it may be that the deception and self-stultification demanded by convention are unavoidable.

Not expressing yourself or expressing a pseudo-self needn't be conscious and needn't be due just to social constraints. There may be something deeper, namely the inability to have fully and freely the kind of emotions that demand expression.

Express Yourself

Inability to express yourself may not be due solely to the confining effects of real or imagined social expectations. Maybe you simply don't know how to express yourself. Possibly you think it's "cool" to be cool. Perhaps your ability to have and to express emotions has been stifled for so long that you're not even aware of having lost it. To use a currently popular phrase, you're not "in touch with yourself." The subject of knowing yourself will be explored in the entire chapter that follows. For now, I want to look at this problem of emotional expression.

Naively, we think of expression of emotion as a cause–effect process: you have an emotion and your behavior issues from it. This may be true of animals and infants, but it is hardly true of those old enough to calculate, control, and feign emotional expression. At best, an emotion *tends* to be given bodily or verbal expression, but contrary to the naive view, this expression may be suppressed, altered, exaggerated, or faked. Often, we cannot express emotions we do have and express ones we don't have. Furthermore, these expressions of emotion can interact with the emotions they express. For example, the intensity of the experience of screaming or crying may amplify the fear or pain felt. The screaming may commit you to feeling scared. Or, if you're acting, the realism of your performance may succeed in getting you to feel what you started to express fraudulently.

Thus, the relation between emotion and its expression is far from straightforward. As we saw in the previous section, it is further complicated by social factors. You aren't supposed to express every emotion in every situation, no matter whom you're with; and you are supposed to express certain emotions even when you don't feel them. For example, you shouldn't express disgust at someone's looks or fondness for someone's wife, and you should express sympathy at funerals, loyalty at college reunions, or enthusiasm at weddings—although you may not happen to feel sad, loyal, or excited. Some emotions get suppressed and others get faked. In general, the expression of emotion has to be tempered so that smooth, unthreatening social interaction can take place without a fuss. But the cumulative effect of all this, whether cultivated as a matter of personal pride ("a man never cries") or of social propriety ("don't upset the apple cart"), is that the emotions themselves become stultified. One simply has fewer and less intense emotions as their expression becomes more curtailed. Eventually, one develops anxiety over being unable to have or to express emotions. The prejudice that expressing (and hence, possessing) certain intense emotions reflects a shameful lack of self-control is an additional inhibitor. It follows that controlling one's emotions indicates an abundance of self-control. I recall how the term *self-control* used to be applied in grammar school to children who "behave themselves." In fact, such self-control implies not self-determination but self-inhibition. Beyond such basics as toilet-training, this idea of self-control is a hoax. Expression of emotion is a person's genuine expression of himself, since the emotion is *his* emotion. It should hardly be the product of calculation; on the contrary, a calculated emotion is hardly genuine.

Knowledge of your own emotions is no easy matter, and the way in which you express them may not help your understanding. A person who always expresses his emotions may only be fooling himself. Constant expression may in fact trivialize the emotions expressed, as in the case of telling everyone how much you adore them. That is, if you express strong emotions all the time, they don't really count for much. In another case, a person may have serious doubts about the genuineness of his own emotional expression, thinking that he only thinks he cares for his dying mother, for example. Although she is such a bother to him, he knows how guilty he would feel if he thought he wanted her to die, so such emotions must be held in check. But this attempt at self-understanding, requiring self-reflection and generating uncertainty, may succeed only in destroying the spontaneity of feeling.

Finally, a person who has an inconsistent emotional pattern may have a difficult time convincing himself that his emotions are real because they change so often. He may think that he should be consistent in how he feels and that irregular outbursts don't really reflect himself. He may find it hard to accept the fact that he is someone who feels different at different times. But why should his feelings have to be consistent?

The same pattern applies to desires as to feelings. Desires don't have to be consistent, either. You're entitled to different moods. You're not obligated to be the same all the time. Of course, if your moods and wants fluctuate too often, you can become hopelessly confused about what you really want. For example, you may do something rash one moment and then wonder later why you did it. It may strike you that whoever did that couldn't have been the same person who's now thinking about it. That's all right. You don't have to be the same all the time.

Knowing what you want is a difficult problem in any case. Of course, what you "really" want is what you want. You can't want something and not want it. But you can wonder why you want it and whether you should. And you can be genuinely ambivalent about it. You may vacillate, but what obligates you to make up your mind?

The Dilemma of Self-Alienation

In the previous chapter, I distinguished between the alienation of nonidentification and that of misidentification. The distinction applies also to self-alienation, though less clearly. We have seen examples of how a person might fail to identify with his actions, with his bodily characteristics, or generally, with what he is for others. This failure of identification may be specific—the person may fail to identify with his long nose—or it may be pervasive— the person may fail utterly to identify with his body or with his actions. Or he may altogether refuse to. Also, he may fail to identify with what he is for himself, especially with his emotions. He may hide them, fake them, or not even recognize them. He may pretend to be what he isn't or not to be what he is, and he may even succeed in fooling himself.

As for misidentification, you might wonder how it is possible to misidentify as your own what is part of you. How could this be misidentification? It could be, at least as a matter of degree. That is, identifying fully and exclusively with only part of what you are means that you are leaving something out. The examples of overidentifying with what you are for others illustrate misidentification. They consist in failing to include what you are for yourself. It is possible, as we saw, to overidentify with what you are for yourself by trying to discount what you are for others. It appears, then, that the two types of self-alienation (nonidentification and misidentification) may go hand in hand.

Oscillation between these two varieties of self-alienation may occur when you are acutely conscious of the difference between your private self and your public self(selves). Sometimes the distinction between what you are for yourself and what you are for others may appear to be in insuperable opposition. There may seem to be no hope of harmonizing the two, perhaps because others can't know you as you really are, or perhaps because you can't be yourself in their presence. Then the dilemma is this: either you feel alienated from your actions and appearance, that is, from yourself as others see you, or you identify with the image that others see, rather than with how you see yourself. Neither of these alternatives is desirable by itself, but there seems to be no way to combine them. So switching back and forth between them may be the only compromise.

You feel either stuck in the world of others or cut off from it. If you feel stuck in their world, an object for their conscious consumption, then your own consciousness may seem to be an insubstantial parasite that has no legitimate place of its own. And if you feel isolated in a world of your own, in which you emphasize your consciousness and subordinate your actions and appearance, then you may feel invisible. For now, the part of you that counts is that least available to others. Besides, by deemphasizing the part of you that others are aware of, you're more or less denying their consciousness—if you are not there for them, then they are there for you.

I wish I knew what to say to enable someone stuck in the dilemma of dual alienation to integrate the direct and indirect ways of looking at himself. If it's a psychiatric problem, then I'm not equipped to solve it. (An implied theme of this book is that certain psychiatric problems are really philosophical—that is, there's nothing pathologically wrong with the person who has the problem.) Perhaps elaborating on the nature of this dilemma can only aggravate it. The analysis itself of the components of the dilemma can make them seem more separate. If you are subject to self-alienation, then being acutely aware of what your choices are can make them seem mutually exclusive. It would be nice to say that it is enough to recognize, calmly and coolly, that a person does have an inner and an outer aspect, and that there is no real problem involved in integrating the two. But how does one go about achieving it?

Clarity of thought and firmness of will are not enough. You can understand fully what is involved in your self-alienation, and why you feel as you do and be determined to do something about it. But what can you do? You realize that you cannot escape your own subjectivity (what you are for yourself) except by rendering yourself less conscious. And you realize that nobody who knows you can know you fully or accurately, for you understand that they can't read your mind, however open and honest you might be. They will always draw conclusions, some faulty, and they will inevitably misinterpret and simplify. What else can you expect? Should you make it easy for them by being nothing more and nothing other than what they think you are? Certainly not. Besides, they'll undoubtedly disagree among themselves. Should you be utterly indifferent to what they think? No, for this will only harden the shell around you.

One solution may be to recognize that others may have the same problem themselves. And if they don't, they should. For if they don't, then they have either succumbed to their image or are trapped in their shells. Surely, it is better to be somewhere between these two states, even if that means wavering between them and wondering how to stabilize and integrate yourself (-selves). Maybe you should share your problem with them, particularly if you care enough about them to care about what they think of you. After all, they are, besides yourself, the source of your problem. And maybe you're the source, partly, of theirs.

Since the dilemma of self-alienation, as defined above, involves reference to others, perhaps we need to learn to appreciate solitude. People today seem to have an almost pathological fear of being alone. They want to be part of what's happening and fear most being left out. The self-alienation involved here, overidentifying with what one is for others, reflects an insecurity about what one is for oneself. Perhaps the fear of facing what one is, for oneself, is based on the fear of losing it. In any case, being at home with oneself seems a necessary balance to needing others.

Who Do You Think You Are, Anyway? 4

You probably have some fairly fixed idea of who you are. It may include what you were and what perhaps you will be. It may even include much of what in fact you are not. No doubt it is affected considerably by what you think others think you are. Whatever it is, who you are is what this chapter is about.

Of course, since I don't know a thing about you, except that you're reading this, I'll have to speak in generalities. You'll have to apply them or reject them.

What a person is is his identity. At least, that's how I'll use the term *identity*. What he thinks he is is his *self-image*. What others think he is is his *image*. What he thinks others think he is is his *secondhand image*.

What is the importance of a person's self-image? Obviously, it is the basis for his self-esteem, if he has any. In other words, what you think you're worth is based on what you think you are. Your degree of self-esteem determines what you're proud or ashamed of, what you're confident of, and what you're afraid of. Your belief in yourself, or lack of it, affects your dealings with others. It is intimately connected with your capacity, or incapacity, for loving and being loved, since thinking yourself worthless renders your love worthless and you worthless for being loved.

Think of all the feelings and emotions built around the self-image: guilt, shame, pride, confidence, ambition, despair. Some are directed to the past and some to the future, and yet they all implicate oneself right now. To feel guilty about something you did is to feel bad about yourself now, not merely then. To feel pride in some past deed is to feel a sense of worth now, not merely of worth then. Analogously, to feel successful when your successes have yet to be achieved is to feel now what you will be later. People count their chickens before they're hatched—and after they've flown the coop.

Your secondhand image deeply affects your self-image. If people accept you, you probably accept yourself. If they don't, it is difficult to accept yourself. It is hard not to think that something is fundamentally and irrevocably wrong with you if everyone else seems to think so.

Your secondhand image doesn't necessarily determine your self-image. A person with what psychologists call *ego strength* doesn't need as much support from others as do those who have less self-assurance. Your self-image can affect your secondhand image. For example, if you think yourself duller than you are, you'll likely think that others think similarly. That is, what you think others think of you can be distorted by an unrealistically high (or low) opinion of yourself. It is easy for your self-image not to correspond with your secondhand image. You may be fooling yourself and others may be fooling you. Or you may be fooling yourself about what they think. Romances and feuds get a lot of mileage out of mutual deception—each has mistaken ideas about the other and about the other's ideas about himself.

A person's self-image is not merely a private matter. Everyone has a social identity that gets incorporated to some degree into his self-image. By *social identity* I mean the whole set of characteristics by which a person is generally recognized and identified in a society. Included are obvious physical features, sex, age, race, class, profession, and nationality. These and other characteristics determine how people perceive each other and roughly what people expect from each other in everyday encounters. Particular groups, membership in which forms part of a person's social identity, provide not only things for people to be but also other people to be them with. Within the confines of a group, terms for encounter and transaction and an atmosphere of relative mutual acceptance are established.

Today, the number of social identity options is overwhelming, for example, in terms of occupation or life style. This abundance of choice seems to have created an unprecedented sense of ambiguity, uncertainty, and malaise. The sheer number can make each option seem dubious, each choice arbitrary, and can create an attitude of, "what difference does it make?" in the swamp of alternatives. In some circles, many of the conventional options have been discredited, such as military service or marriage. Of course, the category of disenchanteds and dropouts has itself been constituted as a group of sorts, complete with identity symbols and norms of behavior ranging from hair style to life style.

Nevertheless, for many, identity has become more and more a private matter, and social identity counts less. As social identity becomes less of a supplier and supporter of private identity,

identity becomes more of a personal problem. As with the problem of meaning, because the problem of identity involves reflection, it is something you face most directly when alone.

I must add, however, the undeniable fact that the quest for identity has itself become a fad. That is, it has become something people do because it is the thing to do, because other people do it. On the other hand, because it pertains directly to oneself, it is more significant than most other fads. Besides, it is not merely a fad, but the inevitable result of a social environment in which the fulfillment of basic needs is taken for granted (by many), and in which most traditional values are no longer taken for granted.

Do You Really Matter?

Who cares what you are? You do. Maybe others do too, but not in the way you do. Suppose we ignore them for the moment. Why should what you are matter, even to you?

I must explain why I have raised such a seemingly bizarre question. I am not asking why anything should matter to you. Presumably some things do, even if there is no ultimate reason why they should (or shouldn't). I am not asking about them, I am asking about you. Why should you matter to you? What I have in mind is this: why should you matter to you over and above whatever else matters to you? Why should you be among the things that matter to you? After all, aren't you simply that which the things that matter matter to?

From your own point of view, you are not just another one of those things that matter. You are not simply in the world with them. The world is your world, from your point of view. You are not there; you are here.

That was from your point of view. From my point of view, the world is my world, and I am not one of the things in it. They, including you, are there; I am here.

Now, if you're not one of the things in your world, for the reason just given, then you shouldn't matter to yourself. You are, rather, the presupposition of anything mattering to you. In a sense, then, you can't really matter to yourself.

In saying that you shouldn't, and can't really, matter to yourself, naturally I don't mean that you should be indifferent to pain, disease, poverty, and other personal misfortunes. After all, they are among the things that matter to you. Similarly, improving yourself, making something of yourself, is valuable as a means of attaining things that matter. For example, exercise and education may enable you to achieve better things for yourself. Their value does not consist in their making a better thing out of yourself; their value is a means, not an end.

I am rejecting the idea that you ought to make something out of yourself because you are, or ought to be, important. Important to whom? I remember amusing myself once at a party by going around asking people to "justify your existence in 25 words or less." Those who didn't find the question offensive saw that they didn't need to justify their existence, to me or to anybody else.

There is another way in which what you are doesn't matter, or shouldn't. Many people place a premium on uniqueness. They think you should be different from everybody else, that you should be an "individual." It makes no difference what everybody else is like. You should be different from all of them. Now I can see the point of being different from everyone whom I don't want to be like, but why should I go out of my way to be different just for the sake of being different? That makes no more sense than being like everybody else simply for the sake of being the same. Isn't it enough to be what you want to be even if it turns out that somebody else happens to be like you? Is there some sort of indignity in not being unique? There is nothing better per se about being different. You can still do your own thing even if it happens also to be somebody else's.

There is nothing inherently good about being special. Furthermore, if there is anything that makes you unique, it is the same thing that makes everybody else unique. How's that for paradoxes? I'd better explain it fast.

Nobody knows what it's like to be you. Right? In fact, this is probably one reason people value uniqueness. Nobody knows, and nobody could ever really know, what it's like to be in your shoes. The reason is not, as you might suppose, that each person is different from everybody else. If that were the reason, it would simply make it difficult for anyone to understand anyone else. Rather, the reason is that nobody else can know you the way you do, "from the inside." Being unique is not what puts you in your unique position. Being you is what does.

Even if everyone were identical, no one would be able to conceive of being someone other than himself. He could imagine being different from the way he is. He could imagine changing. But that's a far cry from imagining not being himself and being someone else instead. The point is that your identity, the set of your salient characteristics, does not define you, since they might be someone else's as well. At least, it is theoretically possible. Your identity does not guarantee, hence does not determine, your uniqueness. Who you are is not merely what you are.

Everybody is unique in that each person has a point of view that no one else does have or could have. This principle for people is analogous to the principle for objects that two objects cannot occupy the same place at the same time. Having your point of view on the world is what it is to be you. That no one else can have it is not an accomplishment but a necessity. Of course, the very fact that makes you different from everyone else does the same for everyone else. So, no matter what you are like, mentally or physically, no one else can know what it's like to be you, to have your point of view. But anyone else can know something very much like that. He can know what it's like to be himself.

You Are Subject

People are persons, not mere things. They have bodies, but they aren't merely their bodies. They, I mean we, have not only physical characteristics but mental ones as well. We are conscious. Our consciousness and our bodies are not disconnected. Sensations occur in your body and are of your body. And it is through your body that you and the rest of the world interact. What you do is done with your body, and what you perceive is by means of your bodily senses.

A person can do much more than act and perceive. Your awareness may extend beyond the present, beyond the here and now. You can think of things going on elsewhere. You can remember the past and envisage the future. In addition to ideas about how the world is, was, or will be, you have ideas about how it ought to be. More specifically, you have desires and intentions that may or may not materialize into action.

Although your awareness extends beyond the here and now in all these ways, still it is centered on the immediate present. For example, to have an idea of something elsewhere implies that the object has a definite spatial relation between what is here in the immediate vicinity and what is somewhere else. You may not know where it is, but it must have some location or other relative to you. Otherwise, it can be only imaginary. Similarly, events past and future must have a definite temporal relationship to what is happening right now. They must have occurred before or after your thought of them, or else they will never have occurred at all. Ultimately, then, to conceive of anything in the world requires conceiving it in relation to what is here and now.

Another way to put the point is this: to conceive of something is in effect to conceive of being in its presence. That means being able, at least imaginably, to be in its vicinity in space and time rather than here and now. Nevertheless, identifying that place and time must be done in terms of its relation to here and now.

Consider, then, how reference is made to things here and now. Ultimately, the only way to refer to something present is to think of it as "this chair," "the chair over there," or whatever. Just describing it as a "chair" is not enough for there might be another chair just like it. Only by singling it out as "this chair here" can unique reference be made. In other words, it must be referred to as the one here and now (if there are several, the reference must be narrowed down further).

Contrary to the myth of objectivity—that there is a universal frame of reference—a person's frame of reference is unavoidably egocentric. To refer to anything in the universe there must be a center of the universe in relation to which reference is made. The idea of a center is, of course, relative. But that's precisely the point—its relativity. I am the center of my universe, and you of yours, but it's the same universe. It can be contemplated only from somewhere and somewhen. Things in it can be referred to only from somewhere and somewhen. That is, here and now. What counts as here and now is relative and everchanging. In this sense, then, I am the center of the universe, if only from my point of view, but it is only from points of view (mine, yours, or whoever's) that the universe can be considered in the first place.

Now we get to the important point in this analysis. If I am aware of things other than myself in relation to myself (here and now), then how am I aware of myself? I don't mean how I am aware of my body, but how I am aware of myself. To be sure, I am aware of my body in a unique way (from the inside) and it is always around, but still I am not it, or at least not merely it. How am I aware of myself as a conscious being, rather than merely as a physical being? An essential requirement, surely, is that I be aware of at least some of my conscious states. And, of course, I have this awareness, in states of what I have been calling *reflexive consciousness.* In those states, I am aware not only of the object of consciousness (for example, my typewriter) but also of the fact of being conscious of it. That's why I call it a "reflexive" state, since it is consciousness of consciousness of something.

As a conscious being, I am a subject of consciousness, or that which is conscious. So, the question I'm asking can be rephrased thus: how am I aware of myself as a subject of consciousness? It seems as if to be aware of myself as a subject, I must make myself into an object of consciousness. After all, it is I whom I am to be aware of. To exploit grammar to formulate the question, how can I be aware of I? I can only be aware of me.

Before trying to answer this question, I want to consider the fact that I (and you, too) am a being in time. What I am is not what

I was or what I will be. I don't mean that I am changing all the time, though perhaps I am, at least subtly. What I do mean is something quite obvious, though by no means trivial in its implications. Look at it from your point of view. What you are, you-now, is what you were at the beginning of this sentence, not what you are now, at the end of this sentence. For you-then is gone, while you-now is here, or was. Whatever you are now is, by the time you finish this sentence, what you were, then.

You are a being in time, and aware of yourself in time. If you focus not on what you are in general but on what you are right now, if you reflect on your present state of consciousness, you must realize that while you are continuing to be, whatever you are at one moment is at the next what you were. From your own standpoint in time, at any moment what you are is distinct from what you were or what you will be. You are continuously passing through time (or is it passing through you? I won't argue the point). Then, how can you ever have an adequate conception of what you are, even right now?   (With this space, I thought I'd give you a little time to find out.) It seems that as soon as you focus on what you are right now, your idea is of yourself then, not of yourself now, reflecting. Your image of yourself may be accurate, but it is necessarily a bit out of date.

Return now to the question: How am I aware of myself as subject? It seems that insofar as I am aware of myself at all, I am aware of myself as an object. That is, what I am aware of does not seem to be identical with what is aware, I. Partly the reason is that what I am aware of is, as stated above, already in the past. My awareness is always a little ahead of myself. A further reason is this: when I am aware of what I just was, specifically I am aware of myself being (having been) conscious of some object, say, the typewriter again. That is, I am aware of myself in the context of being aware of something else. Moreover, I don't have an image of myself. I have nothing of the sort. Rather, I am aware of myself essentially as being that which is aware of the typewriter. I am aware of myself not as what I am but as what I am not. I am aware of myself as not being the typewriter. At any moment, when I am aware of being aware of something, I am aware of myself as not being that (the object of awareness).

In sum, then, I am never quite aware of what I *am*. And to the extent that I am aware of what I am, it is in relation to what I am not, namely the object of consciousness. Only thus can I be aware of myself as subject.

This subject–object distinction is no mere intellectual fine point. Think of what it means to be aware of yourself as subject. As subject, you are what you are by virtue of what you're aware of. For example, if you are looking up at the sky, what you are, looking up at the sky, is in relation to the sky. As subject, you are nothing in itself, but something only in relation to something else. This is true even if that something else is a hallucination. So, if you seem to be seeing an oncoming army of six-foot long red ants, what you are is in relation to them, imagined though they be. That is, a description of you (as subject) giving your present state of awareness must include a description of the object of your awareness.

Think about this. As subject, you are nothing in yourself, save what you are in relation to whatever you're aware of. That's all. Whether it is the public world of physical objects or the private world of dreams and hallucinations, as subject, you are but a transparent presence, a vacuous invader, a parasitical receptacle. As subject, you are utterly insubstantial. You lack even the shape of a shadow.

Of course, you have a body. It is a physical object to which you have a peculiarly intimate and relatively permanent connection. Unlike everything else, it is the one thing that you are aware of from the inside rather than from the outside. But, still it is something that you can, and often in dreams do, dissociate yourself from. It is still an object, even if a very special one. Its presence is not a guaranteed deterrent to the terror of subjectivity.

The "Real Self"

A person's identity is what he is and that, you might well say, includes more than what he is right now. Similarly, his self-image isn't just a reflection on his latest state of consciousness but his idea of what he is in general. I don't deny that a person's identity and his self-image cover more time than a moment. It might even be said that they are, in a sense, outside time, abstracted from time. What someone is, from this standpoint, is not what he is from moment to moment but what he is overall, as a rule. People sometimes talk about their "real self," which their actions, if "genuine," supposedly reflect. And, presumably, their self-image is of this "real self," not of states from moment to moment.

As you might have guessed, I think this "real self" is unreal. Certainly, a person may have a character, a set of traits that are relatively unchanging over time and that are reflected in behavior only from time to time. A person can be kind, for example, even though he doesn't engage in acts of kindness all day every day. But to speak of character traits is not to imply some underlying atemporal self. If there is such a thing, I'm unaware of it.

What I am aware of about myself, in addition to some of my moment-to-moment states, are certain general patterns. They include my beliefs, my desires, my ways with others, my interests, and so on. But these are patterns of myself and my behavior in time, not features of some underlying core outside time.

To be sure, sometimes I might do something unusual for me and later think, "I wasn't myself. That wasn't the real me." But this only means that I wasn't acting the way I normally do, perhaps due to some unusual condition or circumstance I was in. Maybe I wasn't even responsible for what I did. Still, this doesn't imply some atemporal self that normally underlies my actions, but only that I wasn't the way I normally am.

Another possibility is that I had actually changed, if only for the time being. Maybe it wasn't that I wasn't myself but that for the time being I wasn't the way I usually am.

In any case, there is no reason why I *must* be one way. What is to prevent me from changing all the time? Only myself. I am not saying that I (or you) should change all the time. But if I did change all the time, then I couldn't begin to have this notion of my "real self." Nothing would qualify.

Even if you don't change all the time and are thereby able to maintain a fairly steady self-image, don't fall into the trap of supposing that there is some timeless you who underlies yourself from moment to moment. This is not just a metaphysical mistake. It will make you think that what you are is what you have to be. You exist in time. What you are right now may be what you've always been and always will be. But it needn't be. You don't have to, but you *can* change.

Sometimes people talk about "fulfilling" or "actualizing" themselves, and about "realizing their potential." It might be suggested, contrary to what I have been saying, that implied here is an underlying self which only partly "reaches the surface," while the rest is "buried deep inside." I think it's important not to take this talk literally, however well-meaning its intent, which is that a person should become whatever is possible for him to be. Try the same terminology on an oak tree and an acorn. The oak tree is not buried deep inside the acorn, although the genetic potential is, of course, there. Similarly, there is no "real self" buried within a person.

I don't deny that you should have some idea of yourself or your possibilities. We have ideas of all sorts of things. We generalize. We abstract. About all sorts of things, including people. And including ourselves.

Yet there is something special about having an idea of yourself. In this case, the thing the idea is of is the very thing that has the idea—you. What an apple, a book, or a zebra is doesn't need you to think it to be that. But much of what you are is because you think you are. And much of what you "have" to be is really only what you think you have to be. For example, you may be afraid to do something or think you can't. As a result, you don't do it, thereby proving that you can't.

What you are when you are thinking about what you are is someone who is thinking about what he is. What you are when you are thinking about what you have to be is someone who happens to be thinking about what he has to be.

The Trap of Identity

While admitting that each person has his limitations, I have denied the common assumption that for each person there is some underlying "real self" constituting his essential nature—as if there were some concealed "real you" waiting to be made manifest if only you would cut the string and open the wrapper. Or, supposing it's not so simple as that, if only you would solve the puzzle, figuring out what the pieces are and how they fit together.

Something like this assumption was made by Michelangelo, but about marble, not people. With undue modesty, he thought his sculpturing to be nothing more than the uncovering, layer by layer, of the form already contained in the marble. His attitude may have been admirable, but we can't take it seriously. After all, *any* form that Michelangelo chose to uncover would have been concealed in the marble already. Just as no single form is embedded in a chunk of marble, no single form is embedded in a chunk of consciousness. But you may think there is. And that's enough to make it true. It's a self-fulfilling prophecy.

Your identity is what you are, in those respects that matter to you. Your self-image is what you think your identity is. The trap of identity, as I will call it, is this: thinking that what you are is what you have to be.

I am not referring to the fact, common as it is, that you can be mistaken about yourself. I have something else in mind, as illustrated in the following episode. A famed jurist by the name of Learned Mouth is lecturing on the Doctrine of Dirty Feet. His insights fascinate me so much that I want to praise him afterward for his thrilling exposition. When he concludes amidst tumultuous applause, I rush forward to congratulate him. I reach the platform, deftly dodging people in the process, and there he is before me: we are eyeball to eyeball. And then, much to my shame, I clam up. No words issue forth. Embarrassed, I smile meekly and allow others to congratulate him. I think to myself, "What could I have expected? I am still as shy as ever."

If you are shy, then in social situations, you will act shyly. You are likely to be aware of your shyness, all too poignantly aware, no doubt. Shyness is part of your self-image, an unpleasant and perhaps even shameful part. Now the incident described above illustrates how a person can use an element of his self-image to justify or to explain himself (to himself or to others). To explain your shyness by saying, "That's the way I am," is to pretend that that's the way you have to be. No doubt being shy is difficult to overcome, but to give up on the grounds that that's the way you are is to *make* it be true that that's the way you have to be.

Take another case in point. Prim Rose, a young lady reared in the ways of righteousness, believed in God, flag, and motherhood. Her parents made the mistake of sending her to a respectable college for women. It wasn't long before Prim Rose was challenged by her peers on all three of her primal objects of devotion. Needless to say, the challenge took her by surprise. She was shocked by their questioning the unquestionable. She couldn't understand why the others didn't think as she did, and whenever they would probe deeply enough to seek the reasons for her beliefs, all she could say was, "That's what I was taught," or, "That's the way I was brought up."

Prim Rose had no reasons for she had never needed any. What is given and obvious to all needs no reasons. She hadn't arrived at these beliefs; she was implanted with them. She wasn't so much an accepter of these beliefs as, you might say, a carrier of them. Because she was taught them and they were entrenched so deeply, she couldn't help having and continuing to have them.

True, she couldn't help having them when they had never been questioned. But once they were questioned, she was put in the position of being able to evaluate them. Perhaps she would continue to hold these beliefs, but she would do so not because (not as the result) of her training but because (for the reason) of what she had examined. Once she realized that her training made her the way she was, she could no longer use it as an explanation, for now it was up to her either to continue being that way (for reasons of her own) or to change.

What I have called the *trap of identity* (thinking you have to be what you are) is sometimes referred to as *bad faith* or *copping out*. But these labels are subtly misleading. As commonly used, they imply that someone guilty of bad faith is somehow betraying or untrue to himself. I would put it more accurately, if paradoxically, by saying that he is being untrue to himself by being true to himself. That is, he is being true to his self-image by thinking he has to be what he is. He is selling himself out by selling himself short.

I don't mean to suggest that everything about a person he can do something about. Obviously not. You can't change your skin color, though you can change your hair color. You can't change who your parents are, your native country, your age, or (until recently) your sex. You can change your weight, not easily maybe, but no diet will help you lose height. Your abilities are largely natural. That includes both physical and mental ones. Still, it is up to you to find out what they are and to do what you will with them.

Social, economic, and religious characteristics are more changeable than natural ones. To be sure, the opportunities and choices available limit what you can be. In a society in which class is hereditary, the only way for you to change your status would be to change the society itself, or to leave it. Revolution requires supreme commitment, and leaving is not an easy out. Your economic position may similarly depend on matters pretty much out of your control, depending on the type of economic system you are dealing with and at what level you were born into it.

The point I am making about the trap of identity is that precisely when there *is* choice about, say, what you "do for a living," there is danger of coming to think that you have to be what you've chosen to be. Perhaps you have undergone extensive training or have otherwise invested much time and money in a career. A commitment of self or of resources may seem irrevocable, even though you are capable of changing your mind at any time. What keeps most people from doing so is not merely the commitment but the belief that "this is what I do," as if what you do is what you have to do.

It goes without saying, although I am hereby saying it, that economic and educational deprivation, not to mention racial or sexual discrimination, place severe hardships on anyone who might make something of himself. In this section, I have not pretended that there are options where there are none. There are immense political obstacles to opening up full options and opportunities to everyone. I have said only that where these opportunities exist, there is the trap of thinking that what you are is what you have to be (the trap of identity). This is to deny the existence of real options that are closed off only by one's self-conception. A different trap, of a political nature, is the ideological pretense that certain options are available to all, when in fact they are not.

You're Fooling Only Yourself

The trap of identity can be exposed more radically. Simply but paradoxically, I am not whatever I conceive myself to be. Less paradoxically, I am not merely what I conceive myself to be. It doesn't matter what that conception is, for the issue is not with its accuracy or inaccuracy but with the very fact that I have it.

I am a conscious being, a being in time. Indeed, in order to realize that fact, I must be a reflexively conscious being (unlike animals). If you'll pardon a grossly mixed metaphor, I'm in the wake of my past, in the reflection of my present, and in the beacon of my future. I realize this as long as I am aware of myself continuing through time. However, as we've seen, the conception I have of myself is an abstraction outside time. To have this conception, I must think of myself as a thing, albeit a special kind of thing, with traits determined more or less immutably. To say to myself, "This is what I am," is to treat myself as something virtually outside myself, as something "there" for my examination. Whatever the results of the examination, whatever I come to think of myself, it is the very act of examining that inevitably falsifies the results. To engage in such an examination is to seek a conception of the sort of thing I am, all the while neglecting the fact that I am not a thing at all, or at least not merely a thing. I am not something whose character can be established, but someone who establishes his character.

Let me say this a bit differently. Recall that the trap of identity is to think that what you are is what you have to be. In fact, it goes even deeper than that. Whatever I take myself to be can be only what I have been. However accurate and complete this historical self-conception, it is only of what I was and of what I can't help continuing to be. But, insofar as I needn't continue to be what I've been, my conception of myself as continuing to be that is an implicit admission that I can't be anything else. And yet, I can. I can change precisely because I'm aware of what I've been and am thereby in a position to do something about it. Thus, my self-conception is mistaken not because it is misinformed but because it is misdirected. It is directed at what I am rather than at what I've been.

My conception of myself is false or, rather, out of date precisely because it is I who has that conception. Examining myself cannot be done independently of what is being examined, since it is I who is being examined. For one thing, the very fact of being aware of myself as such-and-such is a fact additional to the fact that I am such-and-such. And being aware that I am (have been) such-and-such puts this fact into question, since I am in a position to do something about it. If it is something that is not beyond my control, then to accept it as a fact about myself is to want to continue to be such-and-such. Otherwise, I can accept it only as a fact about what I was.

It is precisely because I am the one who has this conception of what I am that this conception is invalid. Someone else can have a conception of me (or I of someone else) without there being an interaction between that conception and what the conception is of. Unless I know what that conception is, it doesn't affect my own conception of myself. Thus, I can be an object or a thing to another but not to myself, at least not without denying part of what I am. Part of what I am, of course, is a reflexively conscious being capable of changing myself.

Interestingly, some people (including me, by the way) resent being defined by others. "Whatever you say I am, I am not," they insist. They don't want to be reduced to mere objects in the minds of others. One way to avoid this is to be secretive about yourself. Another is to be consciously inconsistent and unpredictable, thereby escaping anybody's definition of you. As you might have guessed, this strategy is self-defeating, since it succeeds in rendering one definable as "evading definition."

In concluding this section, I want to relate what has just been said to the positions of Chapters 2 and 3 on alienation and self-alienation. The dilemma of identification, you may recall, is that one of the two types of alienation is unavoidable. You either fail to identify with something outside yourself, or you falsely identify with it. Clearly, the reason for this dilemma is that identification, as an attempted relationship between yourself and something else, requires defining yourself in objective terms. Since you are not merely objective but subjective, such definition is doomed to failure.

Self-alienation is the inevitable result of imagining yourself to have an objective essence, for this requires treating yourself as an object capable of being completely defined. You are not such a thing. If you treat yourself in this way, if you overidentify with what you are for others (or with what you've been), then you are misidentifying as yourself what is only part of you. You are leaving out what you are for yourself, which always transcends any prior conception.

On the other hand, if you recognize all this and make a conscious effort not to overidentify with what you are objectively (that is, what you are for others and what you have been), you can easily underidentify with this, pretending that it isn't you at all. In the previous chapter, we considered such cases as failing to identify with your body or with your actions. The result is a sense of dissociation with what you are objectively, as if that has nothing to do with what you "really" are. This leads, as we saw, to a sense of utter separation from others, since what they are aware of can never be the "real" (subjective) you. The only way to strike a balance is to recognize the limits of any self-conception.

The Sense of Self

To have a self-image is to be deluded about oneself, at least if it is taken as final. If its reference is to some imagined self that transcends the bounds of time, it is sheer fancy. If its result is to foreclose any future change in the name of necessity, it is sheer folly. Nevertheless, to recognize this about one's self-image is not to eliminate it. Maybe eliminating it is not necessary anyway, and seeing its silliness is enough. In any case, the fact is that we have self-images. It is a fact worth explaining, so I'll try.

Why do we draw conclusions about ourselves? That's what we're doing, after all, when we abstract from the moments of our lives some overall self-conception. Perhaps it is just a special case (and a central one) of our demand in general that things make sense. Perhaps it is a part of our general resistance to indefiniteness, ambiguity, and uncertainty. We want to have a clear snapshot of what is fuzzy, changing, and partly concealed. If this is our demand, then no wonder we cannot be content with the knowledge that we exist and that we are the way we are but don't have to be.

Part of the explanation, no doubt, is other people. People judge each other. We classify and evaluate one another. Therefore, each person is subject to the classification of others, just as others are subject to his. These classifications draw many lines of distinction: physical, aesthetic, social, political, economic, and psychological. Each person is in the position of knowing that everybody judges everybody in all these different respects. Even if people decided to call a truce to this war of the words and agreed to regard each other as equals in spite of their differences, there would likely be those who would refuse and who would be classified by everyone as refusing and as disagreeable. Then the classification game would continue as before, with some people recognized as agreeable, some as not.

The common practice in all sectors of modern society to categorize and evaluate people makes each person conscious of what others think of him. For he knows that he has an image. Of course, there is no single such image, but one per person who knows him. His own image of this image is thus a composite, a simplified synthesis of others' images of him, real or imagined. Needless to say, his secondhand image, the introjection of others' images of him, affects and is affected by his self-image. What he thinks of himself is subject to modification in light of what he thinks others think of him, and what he thinks others think of him is affected by what he thinks of himself. If he shudders to think of what others think of him, he can try to change what they think. If he is afraid of their finding out what he's really like, he can try to manage the impressions he makes. If he can't manage these impressions adequately, he could pretend that he isn't making them. Or, he could deny that others are competent to draw conclusions about him. Or, he could come to believe that the person they know isn't really himself.

Perhaps even more fundamental than the social basis for self is a psychological one. What follows is general and biased but plausible enough to be said. I am going to try to describe something that is extremely complicated (and little understood) in a relatively simple way.

An infant is wholly dependent on others, particularly his mother. He has no sense of autonomy or of competence. On the other hand, he has no sense of the absence of these qualities, for he has no sense of self at all. For him, the world is neither dangerous nor friendly—it just is. To be sure, he reacts to things, he laughs or cries, but he has no differentiated conception of the things he reacts to. Gradually, through processes but dimly and vaguely understood by developmental psychologists, he comes to have a sense of objects as things distinct from himself, which exist even when he's not perceiving them, and which, though distinct from himself, he can manipulate. He has an idea of other people, among them his mother whom he depends on most, his father, brothers, and sisters. Slowly, as his sense of things and of other people develops, and as his sense of his own body does too, he begins to realize his capacity to affect the world, including other people, and for other people and things to affect him. His sense of security depends both on what he can do and on what he can expect. Psychological growth requires both an expanding set of relatively confident abilities, together with a recognition of their limitations, and at the same time, an enlarging awareness of what is going on and of what it means to the child.

This account is highly simplified. I can't be dogmatic about it, but I take something like it to be true. The philosophical observation I wish to make about it concerns the relation between one's sense of self and one's conception of everything else:

To have a conception of the objective world requires, and is required by, having a conception of one's subjective self.

There is a reciprocal or polar relationship involved here. To have a conception of things I must think of them as not being me, or states of my mind. And to have a conception of myself, I must think of myself as not being them. In short, I must distinguish between my experiences and the objects of those experiences.

Moreover, to think of those experiences as mine, I must be able to contrast them with the experiences had by others. This means having the idea of experiences that I don't have. And to conceive of others as being conscious, as not mere things, I must think of them as being fundamentally like myself. In this way, I can have the idea of objectivity, of things that can exist without my experiencing them and of their being experienced without my doing so. But to think of things as being outside of me and to think of others as not being me is to think of myself as not being them. My awareness of the world and of the people and things in it involves distinguishing them from me. I am aware of myself (as subject) as not being in that world, although I am aware of myself as being affected by and affecting it. And, I am aware also of being there (as object) for others, of being in their world(s).

I am suggesting, then, that underlying a person's self-image is his sense of self, which develops and is constituted in the way just described. Your self-image includes the various qualities you attribute to yourself. It defines what you are in particular. But you must first have a sense of what you are ascribing these qualities to: yourself. Your sense of self is the core of your self-image.

Your sense of self is of existing over time with experiences past, present, and future. Your memories, for example, presuppose the thought of having had experiences, conceived of as yours and as past. Similarly, your desires and expectations include an idea of experiences not yet had, conceived of as yours and as future. In contrast to your sense of self there is, as stated above, your awareness of the world outside you, and of others who experience it too, each other, and you.

To appreciate what this sense of self encompasses, try to imagine a situation in which it is lacking. Perhaps you have even been in such a situation. Suppose your experience of the world were haphazard and chaotic, with gross spatial, temporal, and qualitative discontinuities. It would be something like a film with many flashbacks, flashforwards, and general changes of scene occurring at an unfathomable rate. Perhaps you've seen such a film and were totally confused. If your experience of the world were like that, there would be an unfortunate difference: you wouldn't be able to say, "It's only a movie." The theater, lights, seats, audience, and the world into which you reemerge when the movie is over are not part of the movie. Everything is part of the world.

An all-embracing chaos would surely overwhelm your cognitive faculties. Your experience would be utterly fragmented. Nothing would make any sense, for you couldn't put the pieces together. Unlike assembling a jigsaw puzzle, you would be at your wit's end even trying to figure out what the pieces are. Your memory would be swamped in more confusion than when you hear ultramodern music, see an absurdist drama, or have a wild dream.

Whether this chaos were the world's fault or your brain's, you couldn't maintain a sense of self. You would be disoriented, lost, and confused. You would not know what was happening from one moment to the next, being unable to keep track of the past or anticipate the future in its broadest outline. You wouldn't know which way is up.

You'd be unable to keep track of your own past experiences, for how could you tell whether you were remembering them or fabricating them? You couldn't, if the world would never confirm your suspicions or alleviate your doubts. You couldn't maintain an ongoing conception of the world and your relation to it, a sense of interaction with it, inasmuch as your experiences and abortive actions would never mesh with the world. Similarly, you couldn't develop a sense of connection with the future, for you could in no way anticipate, let alone plan, anything. You would thus be stranded in the present, where, in isolation from a coherent picture of past and future, fact and fantasy merge. There would be no way to distinguish what is from what was or will be, or from what isn't at all.

If you were in such a chaotic state—and some people are—you would be totally lost, utterly mystified about where, when, or who you were. You might even be unable to raise such questions. If you have never been in such a state, it is difficult to imagine being in it. It is also difficult to appreciate how amazing your normal state is. You emerged from your mother's womb having had no experience of the world, but having enough mental and physical equipment to figure it out some—with a little help, of course. It is hard to appreciate that your ability to put the pieces together is not automatic or guaranteed. If ever you lose that ability, when and if it returns you'll appreciate it.

Your sense of self is precarious. Having it is to maintain a certain relationship with the world and with other people. It requires having a conception of things in the world as distinct from your experiences of them. It requires that things behave fairly consistently. It requires that you realize that you can interact with things in perception and in action and with people in communication. It is only having a general sense of self, of being in these relationships with the world, that you can even begin to have a sense of identity, of who you are in particular.

I want now to crystallize the thoughts of this chapter. Your self-image is seemingly of what you are. It is illusory insofar as what you are is thought to be some underlying "self," for there is no such thing. That is, there is no atemporal, unchanging "real you" hiding behind your thoughts, feelings, and actions. Otherwise, your self-image can be only an image of what you were, or what you imagine yourself to have to be. It cannot include what you will become, if that is taken as necessary, for that is a matter of choice, not of introspection. And, insofar as you are a subjective being in time, your self-image can never be complete or up to date. It can't even include the experience you're having right now. Thus, to have a self-image and to be committed to it is to limit yourself in the way that only an object can be limited.

Your sense of self is the core of your self-image, but it does not justify thinking of yourself as a thing. It is not the sense of being a thing at all, but of being related to the world and to things in the world. Being in this relationship is essentially what you are, and this is a relation in consciousness. That is, upon reflection you are aware of yourself as subject (as that which has states of consciousness) in relation to the world as object (as that which you are conscious of).

What you think your identity is, no matter what it might be, cannot adequately define you. It is a betrayal of yourself to think that it does—and a metaphysical mistake. You might have found this to be utterly shocking. I tried to cushion the blow at the outset by arguing that from your point of view you don't matter. Rather, from your point of view you are what things matter to. So don't take yourself so seriously!

That's easier said than done. Doing it is the subject of the next (and last) chapter.

The Fringes of Freedom 5

You are a fluke of the universe. Nobody put you here. Nobody put it here (it's a fluke, too). But here you are.

By the time you realize you're here, you're mired in other people's illusions. You're told how you got here, what's been going on in your absence, and what you're supposed to do now that you've arrived. You've learned the rules and the ropes. Perhaps you've learned not to ask any questions—except those already answered.

Things are different now. You used to accept acceptability. Not any more, since, for one thing, you're reading this book. You're trying to break out of the straitjacket of society's sanity. Unmasked, the world appears fresh and frightful. However the world appears, the basic fact is simply that it's there. And here you are, not knowing why and not sure there is a why. The human ascriptions of rhyme and reason seem nothing more than wish and whimsy. Reflecting, you realize that there is no place to go. As for yourself, you are always more than what you've been, and that extra is up to you. In this there is a frightful freedom.

I want first to qualify this discussion of freedom with the proviso that it will have to ignore the political dimension of freedom. There would be far too much to cover: rights, obligations, law, authority, democracy, ideology. It's a bit embarrassing for me to have to ignore all these things, for the tone of this discussion would suggest that political freedom already exists in full. That is, I talk as if you were free to do with your life what you will, when, in fact, there are objective political limitations. I certainly do not mean to suggest that political factors are irrelevant to personal questions of meaning, identity, and freedom. The problem is that I know of no way to incorporate these vast political matters conveniently into this discussion. And, I am sure there are those who would reproach this discussion precisely because of its apparent political presuppositions. To them I can say only that the questions I'm dealing with can't wait, and that political action presupposes answers to them.

Not only do political factors limit a person's possibilities, they also limit his awareness of them. Prevalent ideologies and practices pervade one's education and upbringing and thereby affect one's idea of worthwhile and feasible ways of life. So, certain possibilities get automatically excluded from consideration, while others appear seductively appealing. This is not the place to examine the workings of these restrictive processes. All I can do is warn you to watch out for them.

Self-Liberation

If there is anything to be free from, it's your "self." The intellectual reasons for this were given in the previous chapter. What about the emotional implications? You have nothing to be proud of, and nothing to be ashamed of. The only thing you can be proud or ashamed of is yourself (otherwise, you fall into the alienation of misidentification), and your self is what you have been until now. It's the "ex-you." Pride and shame, then, are not directed at what you are now.

I used to have the occasional experience of recalling some embarrassing event and of feeling ashamed of myself for what had happened. Perhaps I had made a fool of myself or had failed dismally at something or had been seen with my pants unzipped. It didn't matter. The feeling I had in flashing back to such moments was one of utter disgust with myself. Eventually, however, I came to realize that (a) no one else cared except me, and (b) that was me then, not me now. Today, when I recall some awkward moment, I feel so detached from what happened then that I can only smile with amusement. One thing I can say for myself is that I'm consistent. My attitude about those things that most people would feel proud of is that they are just things that happened. They may be pleasant to recall, but they have no bearing on my opinion of myself. They're just memories. I have good ones and bad ones, but memories are all they are.

If you're one of those guilt-ridden types, maybe you're wondering how I feel about those terrible things I must have done. Let's assume I have done such things. The question is, how do I feel about them? The answer is that I have no pangs of guilt whatsoever. I can't even remember the last pang I had. I don't lack such feelings because I'm incapable of recognizing the wrongness of certain deeds. Rather, I don't draw the conclusion that there is something wrong with me now because of what I have done in the past. At most, there was something wrong with me then and that doesn't justify feeling guilty now.

I'm not advocating a policy of irresponsibility, but as some unknown wise man once said, "Don't cry over spilt milk." Not only are such retrospective feelings useless, they refer to something that was, to the "ex-me." I see no reason why how I feel now should depend on what I think of what I was. I see no reason why what I am now or what I am worth now should automatically and irrevocably be stuck with the stamp of what I was. I bear no stigmas and wear no medals. Also, to be consistent, I hold no grudges.

The future is another thing. Unlike the past, it is something you can affect. Make of it what you will. But as for the past, it's come and gone. You don't have to forget about it, but don't limit what you are to what you've been. You're not the mere object that your self-image would have you be and that the feelings of pride, shame, and guilt are directed at. Thus, to have them is to be victim of the self-alienation of misidentification.

Probably the overwhelming obstacle to being free from your "self" is other people. Without them, you would have no image. You'd have nothing to live up to, no reputation to maintain, no face to save. You wouldn't need to manage the impressions you make. You'd have no mask and therefore no problem with its fitting. But there are other people. They pass judgment and have expectations. And they in turn are judged. Indeed, all human interactions seem to involve an implicit process of mutual judging and impressing. People impute selves to each other, so it's no wonder that they feel obliged to be stuck with their images. What would everybody think if I didn't continue to be the sort of person they know me to be or want me to be? As long as I ask that question, I'll continue to be precisely that sort of person.

The alternative is to realize that there is nothing for people to know you to be. You may still play roles and put on airs, but you won't identify with your image. You may even feel alienated in interaction, since you don't identify with what people take you to be. I've had this experience for some time now, and all I can do is try to explain how I feel if I think explaining is worth the trouble. If not, then I pay the price of feeling alone and separate from the situation. Escaping your image takes effort, practice, and patience, but it has the added merit of enabling you not to pass judgment on others.

Autonomy and Identity

Freedom–from does not equal freedom–to. So you might wonder if freedom from your "self" precludes being able to do things for yourself. It might seem that not being wedded to an idea of what you are would render you confused about what to do for yourself and reduce you to passivity.

In fact, it is one thing to have an idea of what you are (were) and another to be able to act for yourself, to have autonomy. The two are related but different, and the difference is important. Having a clear-cut self-image in no way guarantees autonomy. Take the case of the young woman who marries an ambitious fellow for security, the price being to serve him. (Or is it a price, if she prefers not having to make her own decisions?) Her lack of autonomy goes hand in hand with her alienated identity. She defines herself primarily as her husband's wife, and his achievements, as the result of this false identification, are derivatively hers. There is the different case of the woman who controls her husband, while yet identifying with his achievements. Playing a dominant role, not a kowtowing one, she acts autonomously, and yet her identity, too, is alienated.

The first woman illustrates the case of having a clear sense of identity and yet being unable to do things for oneself. In fact, one's ineffectuality may in part define one's identity. People who feel utterly helpless see themselves all too clearly as slaves or as mice.

On the other hand, it is also possible to feel fully competent, to be able to make decisions and be effective with others, and yet to have a very unclear self-image. Self-alienation is all it takes. A good example is the disenchanted business executive who feels that what is being expressed in his actions and re-spected by others isn't really himself. He may be successful by ordinary standards, but his dreams have come true only along with disillusionment. For him, the price of autonomy was a false self.

Although autonomy and identity are distinct, I don't mean to suggest that they are unrelated. As an extreme example, a person may feel utterly insignificant because nothing he does matters to anybody and no one ever notices him. He may lose his very sense of being and feel as if he is nothing at all. Feeling invisible, he may desperately do things that guarantee others' noticing him, such as being obnoxious or even violent. Another approach may be to moan about his problems to others, to become an object of sympathy. In some cases, paranoia is the only way to cope with this sense of insignificance. By fabricating an elaborate scheme of how the world is out to get you, there can be no doubt of your cosmic importance. The plot that everyone is party to insures the firmness of your existence precisely by threatening it.

Although autonomy and identity are related, what kind of autonomy does a clear-cut, positive self-image really provide? If you know what you are and you're glad to be that, you act with confidence and assurance. But is this the same thing as acting autonomously? In fact, you're riding the crest of the past. You're acting not from within but from inertia. You're doing what you're doing because of what you are, and that is nothing more than what you've been and what, through lack of reflection, you'll continue to be. To be this kind of autonomous is to be a prisoner of the past.

I'm not saying that you should make a continual conscious effort to change. That's impossible and hypocritical—you would eventually realize that what you always are is someone always trying to change. What I mean, instead, is that you should avoid developing and maintaining a fixed, definite image of yourself, as if that's what you have to be. The easiest way to keep your self-image fluid and the best way to avoid the fetish of always having to change is not to worry about it. Let yourself be. You don't have to be anything in particular (at least within practical limits), and let others think what they may.

It is not easy to forge ahead without resting on the laurels of the past. Having a self-image that feels comfortable is better than being anxious about it, but not needing one is even better. Not having to be something means you can be anything, even what you've never been before; there is always room for choice, but having a fixed self-image takes up a lot of it.

Not having to be anything in particular keeps things wide open. I'm not saying you should be like a cork bouncing around in the ocean. True, the cork manages to stay afloat through it all. But unlike the cork, you're not helplessly subject to stimuli; you can consciously react to them. What's more, you can initiate action. Still, there's merit to the corny cork analogy. Autonomy doesn't mean blotting out the world around you. The cork, though anything but autonomous, teaches change. There's no reason to hold off from the world by holding onto yourself. Holding onto yourself won't prevent you from getting bounced around. And the irony is that there is nothing to hold onto anyway, except the mirage of past as present.

So far, I have tried to show that autonomy, doing things for yourself, does not require acting from your self-image. Only pseudo-autonomy lets your future be determined by your past. Autonomy does not exclude openness but invites it. Autonomy, as we'll see next, does not equal control.

Out of Control

Do you really think you have things under control? Don't count on it. No matter how confident you are, how free you feel, or how independent you think you are, you're only kidding yourself if you think you have things under control. You may admit that you can't take everything into consideration or anticipate everything that is about to happen. Things are much too complicated for that. Still, you say, most of the time you're in charge of what's happening. You've managed to rescue yourself from society's pliers. You run your own life. Or so you think.

In fact, you don't have even yourself under control. That would mean controlling every state of your consciousness. And that's impossible. Each act of controlling your own consciousness would itself be a further state of consciousness. This further state would be either in or out of control. If in control, then there would have to be a still further state controlling it. This still further state would be either in or out of control depending on whether there's a further state controlling it. Sooner or later, some state couldn't be controlled.

In actual fact, there are far too many mental goings-on at any given moment for very much to be under control. So it is both theoretically and practically impossible to be fully in control of yourself, let alone of anything else. Far from it. Just try to contemplate yourself right now. Each introspective glimpse of the fleeting episodes of experience is itself a further episode. Thus, total control is out of the question.

If you think about it, you realize that very little of what happens in your life is your own doing. Some of it is the doing of others, the rest unintended altogether. These unintended happenings are sheer chance, relative to what you could have known. I mean they may not be chance in some ultimate sense, but in fact, you couldn't have expected them. Think of how you met each of the people you know. Was it intended or happenstance? Think of the experiences you have had and the things you have learned. How many did you anticipate? Moreover, when I just asked you to think of these things, what determined the particular ones that you thought of?

There's not much you can do about your life; it's mostly outside your control (and outside anybody else's as well). If you find this difficult to accept, perhaps you're focusing your attention on your plans and schemes, on the things that you prepare for, deliberate on, and carry out. These purposive phases of your life certainly get the most attention, but that doesn't mean they count the most. Besides, think of all the unexpected intrusions on your intentions.

Try to recount what has happened to you in the last 24 hours. How much, really, was planned, either by you or by anybody else? Now, you may remember best those things that were planned, things that you were "going to do today." But, just because they were supposed to happen, don't neglect everything else, all the inner and outer distractions, the people you saw, the sounds you heard, the traffic light that didn't turn red when expected to, thereby enabling you to get where you were going a minute earlier than you otherwise would have. Everything must be taken into account for you to appreciate the chanciness of things: the time you waste, the time you save, the delay here, the shortcut there. Maybe you hit a run of green lights, and you pass the spot where a hitchhiker who would have robbed you hasn't yet appeared. He gets someone else instead. Meanwhile, you run out of gas two miles farther from town than you would have had you hit red lights instead of green. The driver who passes and ignores your plight has problems of his own, a man with a gun hidden from your view.

Relative to our limited knowledge, almost everything that happens is chance, from the most trivial to the most significant. Think of the thousands of accidents that have occurred today but didn't happen to you. Think of the good things that do happen. Somebody recommends to you just the right book or introduces you to just the right person. You just happen to open the newspaper to the page on which a unique job opportunity is advertised. You miss the plane that is hijacked. You walk in the door just as that important phone call rings. You walk out the door, slam it, and realize you forgot your keys—but you also forgot to lock the door. Concentrate on the idea that so much is unexpectable. Pay attention to the things that happen in the next few minutes, and you'll see what I mean.

Perhaps what is behind the ideal (a dubious one, as we'll see) of total control is the image of the self or ego running the show. Whether the imagined model is of a little man inside, a telephone operator, or a movie director, the central idea is that what brings an experience to consciousness is a process of selection and that therefore there must be a selector. But to suppose that there is a selector is to think that each state existed somewhere else before being selectively brought to the fore of consciousness. I'd like to know where. Moreover, if there is this inner selector, then he (it) must have states of consciousness that make the selections on the mental jukebox. Surely, that's absurd.

In addition to this model of the controlled mind, there is also the appeal of power. Some people feel that asserting power is equivalent to demonstrating their significance. Apparently, they think they have to prove something—that the world is no obstacle. Conning others, who are part of the world, is the means of confirming this. The trouble with power-hunger, apart from its ultimate frustration, is the faulty idea behind it. The world is no obstacle, and there is nothing opposed to it for it to be an obstacle to. You don't have to combat it. To think that you do is to regard yourself primarily as an object that is validated in proportion to how much it affects everything else. The insecure logic involved seems to be this: "The more I control the world, the less it controls me. The less it controls me, the more secure I am. Therefore, the more I control it, the more secure I am."

Total control is not only impossible but undesirable. Some things need to be controlled, like violence and disease, but only some. In most cases, control (like the so-called self-control demanded in schools) is self-repression, keeping things away or holding them down. This is the order of rigidity. Making things happen, instead of preventing them, requires creativity. The discipline associated with creativity is not the order of rigidity but the order of growth. In order to grow, any system must be so organized that it can benefit from integrating experiences accumulated from the past. The sort of order needed for such learning is flexible. Otherwise, nothing new could be accommodated in the present.

Speaking of creativity, I recall various psychological studies that have shown moments of creation to be spontaneous, not rehearsed. And what would you expect? If a person knew in advance what his forthcoming creation was going to be, it would hardly qualify as a creation. Nevertheless, these spontaneous moments are no mere matter of luck. The person who has such moments must be in a position to have them, and that requires patience, practice, and discipline. The only originality that occurs in a vacuum is randomness.

The reason some people seek repressive control is precisely what is wrong with too much control. Many people simply like to know what is going to happen. They want things to be predictable. This need may be based on a quest for power or be grounded in a fear of risk and danger. Whether control worshippers seek sovereignty or security, they're paying the price of missing the boat. They refuse to let things happen, most of which are not dangerous and many of which are pleasant surprises. Among these surprises are those occasional moments of amazement or astonishment that seem to justify all the rest.

Being for Real

Autonomy (being free) does not equal control. Perhaps what it means is being willing and able to express yourself in action, to "be who you are." But what does that mean? If you take "be who you are" literally, then it's a rank triviality. Who else can you be? Interpreted, the least that it means is that you should be free to be who you want to be, that you shouldn't be forced into being what someone else wants you to be. It suggests, further, that what you want to be should be your authentic desire, not a concession to convention or convenience. I think we can agree that these are at least part of what is meant by "being who you are" and of what is involved in being autonomous. But there is more.

"To thine own self be true." Not a bad idea if you have a self to be true to. And yet the "self" you have is not you. It is only what you have self-image of, and there is nothing, we have decided, that corresponds to that. So, being true to yourself can only be being true to your self-image. That's nothing more than reinforcing your prejudices about yourself. What's being true to yourself about that? There is nothing to be true to. Therefore, being true to your "self" is in a sense being untrue to yourself. That is, being true to yourself requires refusing to be true to what you falsely think you have to be because you are. Appealing to "the way I am" when you don't have to be that way is to fall into the trap of identity. Being true to yourself, in the only legitimate sense, means recognizing that your options aren't automatically closed, based on what you've been. Being true to yourself means, therefore, realizing that there is nothing to be true to.

Naturally, you shouldn't exercise every option that you recognize. On the other hand, recognizing your options but never acting on them is worse than not recognizing them at all. Of course, nobody fully exercises even the options he wants to. We all operate to some extent on momentum and inertia, as framed by social and personal dictates. Whenever you realize that you're coasting, however, you've opened the door to doing otherwise or, for that matter, doing the same consciously. Awareness of what you're doing creates new options that further awareness can create still more of. Such awareness broadens your boundaries, and while boundaries can't be eliminated entirely, there is no limit to the broadening effect of self-awareness.

Although self-awareness opens options, it does create dangerous complications. There is more and more for you to think about and greater and greater responsibility as you try to take over the controls from your autopilot. This can be downright terrifying. You may yearn for the ability to take the old things for granted: the way you used to be, the certainty of society's norms, the rightness of what you thought right. What's more, the demand on your nervous system is greater, possibly producing information- and decision-overload.

Fortunately, some things do work automatically, such as your heart, your lungs, and your digestive system. Convenient, isn't it? Imagine what it would be like if you had to operate these systems consciously. It would be arduous, to say the least, keeping track of your innards and making sure everything was working properly. You'd soon wish you could delegate authority to your autonomic nervous system so that you wouldn't have to bother with all those details. Should a fear of being untrue to yourself deter you from wanting to do that?

That's a good question. For us, staying alive is more or less automatic. Suppose life had to be chosen constantly. Suicide would be much easier. As things are, it's much easier to die accidentally than on purpose. Perhaps the truly authentic person is one who takes his life into his own hands at all times. I'm glad I can't do that.

By the way, maybe you've been wondering what the point is of being authentic. Is the authentic person, the one who is true to his nonself, out to prove something? If to others, then he's not being authentic at all. He's only putting on a mask. If to himself, then being authentic is just a way of satisfying his self-image, in which case the effort would be self-defeating. If authenticity is something to be pursued, then the very pursuit of it is an inauthentic act of self-deception.

As I see it, authenticity isn't a value at all. That is, it isn't something you can shoot for. Rather, it is a characteristic of someone to the degree that he really does make choices instead of living inertially. It's a consequence of conscious awareness of one's own doings. And you can't really try to be conscious. You either are or you aren't. When you aren't, you can't try to be conscious unless you're already conscious enough to see the need to make the effort. On the other hand, if living choicefully rather than inertially becomes an obsession, authenticity turns into a mockery.

What, then, is the relation between authenticity and autonomy? Part of it is recognizing your possibilities. As we discussed in the previous section, you may realize that very little is or can be under your control. That doesn't mean that nothing is up to you. To recognize the illusion of being in control is not to acknowledge control by something else. Your choices are limited but you still have to make them.

Suppose you acknowledge the authority of something else, human or otherwise (divine, political). Still, it is you who acknowledges that authority. It is you who says "Yes" and you who says "No." And to what authority can you confidently say "Yes," considering all the competition among the contending authorities in both the religious and the political spheres? However you may answer, you are the authority of authorities, so you really have no choice but to be your own god and to be your own sovereign. Maybe you're not fully qualified for the job, but then who is?

Think of the extent to which you let others do your thinking for you and otherwise influence you. How long did it take you to realize that this had been going on all your life? Think of the extent to which you live by habit and inertia, doing the same old things in the same old way. Think of all the options that are available to you at any given moment. Even if you're not aware of them, they're still there.

Yours for Choice

Your freedom is no greater than the range of your possibilities. If they are genuine possibilities, then you must be aware of them so that you can choose from them. There is a traditional problem in philosophy about freedom of choice, usually labeled *Free Will vs. Determinism.* The seeming conflict is this: as conscious agents, we have the impression that what we do (some of it, anyway) is up to us—our action is a product of our will, a matter of choice. From a scientific viewpoint, however, everything seems to be determined, to follow laws (known or unknown), to be caused. That includes the physiological states of our brains. Since we have no reason to suppose our mental states to be anything but by-products of our brain's states, we must conclude that they too are part of the vast causal nexus of the universe. Since these mental states include our desires, wishes, and choices, it follows that our mental states cannot be the initiators of our actions. Or so the argument goes.

I'm going to make no attempt to analyze this or other arguments for determinism and against free will. And I'm not going to deal with the counterarguments, either those that try to refute determinism or those purporting to show that free will is not precluded by determinism, that there's really no conflict. Rather, I'd like to show that the whole problem is academic. It's fascinating as a philosophical problem, but it has no practical consequences.

The main thing to understand about choosing is that you can't choose to choose or choose not to choose. You're stuck with having to choose, even if it's only to choose not to. If you're not able to choose, it is either because there's nothing you can do in the situation or because you haven't perceived any alternatives to what you're doing. As soon as you realize that there are other possibilities, you have no choice but to choose from among them, even if that choice is to keep doing the same thing as before.

Suppose you hold the philosophical position that every event is physically caused (subject to physical laws, predictable in principle), and that choice or will is not the cause of conscious human action. Let's suppose you believe that, and I know many philosophers who do. You would still act the same as anybody else, just as they do. You would still ponder your options, make decisions, and welcome or regret the consequences. So what practical difference does your philosophical conviction make? None, it seems.

When the power of the will is challenged, one immediately thinks it is being claimed that the will makes no difference, that a person's choosing to do something has no bearing on its happening. But this is not the implication of that challenge at all. For one thing, even if acts of will are not causes of action but effects, most immediately, of brain states, still it is reasonable to suppose that those brain states, the ones producing acts of will, are different in kind from those that produce what we prescientifically describe as automatic or unconscious behavior. So, the presence of an act of will signals a difference, even if it does not itself make a difference. Thus, acts of will are not irrelevant to the occurrence of actions. They are causally connected, even if not causes, in that they are the inseparable effects of whatever causes those events (actions) that are naively taken to be the effects of the acts of will.

But there is a more important point. Roughly speaking, we have no choice in the matter. That is, we are in the position of facing the future, of being presented with a range of options, and of knowing that certain actions will have (with a certain degree of probability) certain consequences. In short, we find ourselves in situations in which we have no choice but to make choices. We cannot say to ourselves, "As a philosopher, I believe that the will does not causally produce actions. Therefore, I will hereby abandon the exercise of my will." That, in itself, is a self-contradiction.

Instead, we must recognize that the use of the will is the exercise of the limited knowledge that we have—knowledge of ourselves, of the world, and of the relation of the present to the future. In particular, we know certain likely relationships between actions and outcomes. And, we know that making a choice does in fact lead to the performance of the action chosen (unless we are prevented or change our minds). So we have no choice but to choose.

In practice, there are many unknowns about human behavior and limits to how much we can know and think about at a given time. But, even without these practical limitations, in principle we could never know enough so that we wouldn't have to choose and to act. You could never sit back, in seeming philosophical comfort, and pretend to be a mere witness to the cosmic spectacle, while saying that your will is wholly out of the causal picture. As argued earlier, even if it is not a cause, still it makes a difference.

If your will made no difference, it would not be due to the inexorable forces of physical nature. Rather, it would be because something were wrong with you and you couldn't perform any actions. Suppose that for some unknown reason, all of a sudden you no longer did what you intended to do and your every project fell flat on its face. It wouldn't be long before you gave up trying to do anything. In such circumstances, there would be no difference between willing and daydreaming. As things are, however, there is a difference. Unlike daydreaming or idle wishing, willing does matter to what happens and there is no way (nor reason) to alter that fact. However much you know about causes, you're in a position to choose. You don't have the choice not to.

The more you know, the more informed your choices. That doesn't make them easier. Decisions can become difficult if there is too much to take clearly into account, especially if anxiety is mixed in. Also, becoming informed takes time. Sometimes you just have to act.

What Do You Want?

To act, it helps to know what you want. But knowing what you want is not as easy as it might seem. One reason for this was mentioned in the section on "Alien Values" in Chapter 2, that people often want things because everybody else wants them. So they think they want an extra TV set or fancier ski accessories. Or, they think they want to attend operas.

Knowing what you want seems simple. Either you want something or you don't, and if you do you know it. So how can you think you want something but not really want it? The case of alien values illustrates how. Besides, your wants aren't sitting on pedestals waiting to be examined. They come and go, they are clear or diffuse, they conflict with one another. You can want something without thinking about it all the time. You can want something without doing anything about it. You can think you want something because the idea of it somehow appeals to you

—maybe you fantasize about the situation that having it would put you in, or about the accolades you'd receive.

Another source of confusion is your self-image. You have a certain idea of yourself, and you assume that anyone of that sort (your sort) has certain desires. If you're a businessman, you therefore want more money and a better position. If you're a performer, you therefore want stardom. So you want, or think you want, whatever your sort of person is supposed to want.

A slightly different type of confusion is due to "attitude inertia." You want something because you always have. Or, you don't want something because you never have. Either way, you're assuming you have to be the way you've been and you're denying yourself the chance to be otherwise. For example, since early childhood, there were certain foods that I refused to eat. When I finally tried them, I liked them. Inhibition about something may keep you from doing it, even though, "deep down," you wish to. It is easy to pretend that you don't want to do what in fact you would want to do if you weren't afraid of embarrassment or ridicule. These fears can be deepened by habit. The only way to break the habit and overcome the fear of doing something is to do it. I'm sure you've had the experience of doing just that and were amazed, after you did it, that you could have been so anxious about it.

Wanting something isn't merely being in the habit of wanting it. You're always in a position to change your mind or to decide of what mind you really are. Your wants aren't things to be found. Finding out what your wants are is at the same time deciding to continue to have them or to change them. For it is you whose wants they are.

Part of the problem in knowing what you want is knowing how you are. Sometimes, when someone not meaning it asks me, "How are you?", I realize that I don't know how I am. Only if I feel really great or really rotten am I sure of how I feel. If I'm feeling in-between and if no one asks how I feel, I may not even be aware of how I feel. I'm paying attention to something else. Paying attention to how I am may change how I am, or even affect what I'm doing. When you're not clear about how you feel, it seems important to find out. But if you don't wonder, it doesn't matter, does it? Even if how you are is important, it may not be good to think about. Thinking about it may only make you feel worse. But, of course, thinking about it is not something you can decide to do or not to do. Either you do or you don't.

The main thing to realize is that you're never quite what you think you are. When you realize what you're feeling or what you're wanting, what you are now is being in the state of realizing that. You can never quite catch yourself in the act, but only between acts (not counting the act of catching yourself in the act). Trying a little harder won't help any more here than running faster would help you catch your shadow. The reason you're never quite *what* you think you are is that you're never quite *when* you think you are. You're always a step ahead of yourself. Therefore, determining how you are and what you want is not just fact-finding but also decision-making.

Escaping the Present and Finding It

The trouble with thought is its ability to wrest you away from the present. Direct experience requires the presence of the things experienced. Not so with thought. That's the virtue of thought, as well as the trouble with it. Things don't have to be here and now to be thought about. Thought enables you to transcend immediate experience. Abstractly, you can conceive of (or begin to conceive of) the vastness of the world and of time. You thereby realize the smallness of yourself and of your place in the scheme of things. More practically, thought is the basis for plans and the root of much fear, hope, pride, and regret. All human endeavors and emotions that take time or otherwise span time presuppose thought's power to escape the present. Without this power, you would have no worries, but you would also have nothing to look forward to. You would be incapable of anxiety or anticipation.

We can't give up our power of thought, but wouldn't it be nice to get back to the present? Notice that this very question alludes to an imagined future. Indeed, by writing or reading this we are both escaping the present, precisely by thinking about not escaping it. And by saying this, I am escaping from what I had intended to talk about, namely escaping the present, although by so doing I have illustrated the point I was going to make.

The point I was going to make is that the difficulty in trying not to escape the present is that the present itself is continually escaping. It is not something you can try to hold onto. Time marches on. The best you can do is to try to prolong whatever is happening right now. This is not holding onto the present but holding onto what's presently happening. And prolonging it must give way to remembering it, which is to be back in the past. The only way not to escape the present is not to latch onto anything else than what is here and now. Either way, latching on is escaping the ongoing present. Prolonging the present is not preserving it but only stretching it out. The taffy of time will stretch only so far.

It would be imprudent of me to say that the past and future should be ignored. Needless to say, there is much to be learned from the past, and moments yet in the future will become present. It's just a matter of emphasis: what counts ultimately is the present. Let me explain why. If the past matters now, then something must have mattered then. And if the future matters now, it can matter only because of what will matter later. So, it is in relation to past nows and future nows that the past and future matter. The moments at which experiences occur are the moments at which, ultimately, they matter.

I'm not saying, of course, that everything that happens in the present is good, desirable, or worth experiencing. I am saying that for anything to be intrinsically good or desirable, there must be some present in which it is worth experiencing. It can't be worthwhile merely as past or merely as future, except in the secondary sense of being a means to an end or of being something to learn from or to avoid. There is a lack in the life of someone who can only hark back to the good old days or who can only look forward to the tomorrow that never comes.

The mixed blessing of thought enables you to escape the present. By so doing it can make you appreciate things comparatively rather than in themselves. That is, by remembering past experiences and anticipating future ones, you thereby implicitly put the present one on a scale. Is it better or worse than others of the same sort? Is this the most beautiful painting I've ever seen? Is that the finest person I've ever met? Is this a first-rate orgasm? Is that a second-class joke?

Comparisons can provide no ultimate basis for value: if something is better than something else, there must be something good about it (or something bad about the other). It must be better than the other in some respect. If it is really worthwhile, it can't be so merely because something else doesn't match up to it. Not only do comparisons fail to provide an ultimate basis for value, but the act of making comparisons wrenches you from the present. For the comparison you make of your present experience is with those of other times.

Escaping the present needn't be done alone. It is easily done as a joint effort, as illustrated by these conversational snippets:

Where are you from?

What do you do?

Nice weather today.

We met here last year.

Do you know . . .?

I have a cousin from there.

See you next year.

Most conversations consist of small talk, if by that we mean talk used to fill time and to avoid the awkwardness of silence. It is directed not to the immediate concerns or feelings of the conversants but to things people pretend to be interested in, if only mildly. When small talk is the extent of conversation, expression of genuine emotion and serious thought is excluded. Triviality is the order of the day, indifference or feigned emotion its execution.

Generalities and trivialities keep feelings from being focused. Role playing is easier than being yourself and expressing yourself. Cliches are convenient. Revealing yourself is risky. If you feel hostile to the other, you'd rather hide how you feel than hurt his feelings or risk retaliation. If you are secretly fond of the other, perhaps you fear a lack of response or even contempt. Besides, if you keep your distance, it's easy to get away if you have to. If the other person has the same fears and anxieties you do, then moments of intimacy will surely be rare, as the escapist charade continues instead.

Escaping the present—feelings and experiences, persons and things—is the product of thought and is done, it seems, in the name of security. It's the policy of making sure that the wrong thing won't happen, that the right thing will be taken care of, and that the whole process will run smoothly. The trouble with this passion for security is all that it leaves out, all the passing moments.

This passion for security can be described differently. Suppose you ask yourself, "What is now?" This moment? This hour, day, week, year? This lifetime? If you think only in terms of weeks and years, you are motivated by such things as fear and ambition. You're missing out on the moments that life is made of. When you think exclusively in longer terms, then it is difficult to feel that you're moving. The units of the time scale are too large. Like faraway mountains, the past and future don't recede or approach, even though you're speeding along.

Sometimes it takes courage to face the present, or maybe it's faith (*faith* is not one of my favorite words). Either way, you have to be confident not so much in yourself as in the world. Of course, there are dangers, and there is no reason to court them excessively. You don't have to be a daredevil to enjoy life. On the other hand, worry and anxiety do more harm than good. Since most of what happens, good or bad, is beyond your control, there is no point in worrying about everything. Also, there is no point in worrying about whose doing these happenings are (yours, others', or nature's). What counts is not who does what but what happens.

The time is now. It just takes tuning in on. I can't tell you how to do it. That's for you to figure out in your own way. All I've tried to do is help you push aside certain roadblocks, which requires recognizing them for what they are.

The first roadblock was the demand for meaning. There is no way to make the moments of life add up to something, but there is no real need to. For it is at particular moments when this seeming need is felt. There is no possibility of a final endless moment when everything comes together and stays there. Ironically, seeking the meaning of life prevents a person from finding what ends that quest. What ends it is not an answer but the elimination of the question. That happens when you realize that what you're looking for is nowhere to be found—it's here already.

The second roadblock was actually a reappearance of the first. This was the need to identify with something, to get a sense of personal importance by annexing oneself to something of unquestioned importance. Apart from the questionability of the importance of things people identify with, there is the question of identifiability. Identification with something cannot succeed— you are you and it is it. And once you realize that mystical unities are not possible, no longer do you need to feel that anything is missing if you don't identify with something. So, the alienation of nonidentification is based on the illusive hope of identification.

The third roadblock results from getting past the second. Once you realize that you have nothing to identify with but yourself, there arises the problem of defining that. The dilemma is that any definition is of what you are for others or merely of what you have been, while what you are for yourself escapes definition. That is, defining yourself is to render yourself into a mere object. Overidentifying with what you are for others precludes identifying with what you are for yourself. On the other hand, identifying only with what you are for yourself, with yourself merely as subject, cuts you off from the world. You're a ghost of your former self. The third roadblock is a dilemma, and its clearance dissolves the dilemma. That is, you must see that the situation isn't either/or. You are both what you are for others and what your are for yourself.

The fourth and final roadblock is your "self." Even after you've recognized your inner and outer aspects, the quest goes on for a self-definition that explains both. No self-definition can be adequate, because there is no underlying "self " for it to be adequate to. Any self-definition, if taken as final, hides the fact that you are always ahead of yourself. Not only is there no "self " to be found, but the self-image that pretends to reflect it is always out of date.

Notice that each of these four obstacles is founded on reflection. Each time you're blocked by one of them, you may be inclined to think, Socrates notwithstanding, that the examined life is not worth living. The process of reflecting on life seems to impose unreasonable demands and to focus a person on himself, thereby creating anxieties not easily dispelled. You may yearn for the unrecoverable innocence of unreflectiveness, in which things were taken for granted and nasty questions weren't asked. I have tried to let the process of reflection run its course (not that it ever ends). Going part of the way, you feel a certain need for meaning and identity. Going further, you realize that these needs cannot be met, thanks to that reflexive nature of yours that created them. But continuing on, you realize that these needs don't have to be met. Reflection reveals that they are not genuine needs. So, while reflection initially demands something permanent (in the world and in yourself), and subsequent reflection recognizes the futility of such a demand, still further reflection reveals the fact that yielding to this demand is an attempt to evade the very process of reflection that imposed the demand in the first place. As a reflective being, you are always a step ahead of yourself, and therefore cannot expect a fixed, permanent, and absolute basis for living.

Being ahead of yourself means that there is nothing for you to be true to. What you are is not a foregone conclusion. Possibilities remain open, and it is up to you to be open to them. That doesn't mean you can't be selective. Quite the contrary, selecting is always yours to do. Just don't let the demands for meaning and identification, the dilemma of self-definition, and the image of self get in the way. Apart from the illusions that created them, these demands for meaning also wrest you from the present by demanding a justification of the past and/or an obsession with the future. Like mountains in the distance that seem stationary though you're speeding along, the past and the future, when abstracted from the present, seem to have permanence and importance in contrast to the fleeting present. And yet, whatever meaning and importance they can rightly have is in relation to the present, fleeting though it be. There is no escaping the present, for we're moving with it. Always, now is the time.

If eternity is taken to mean not infinite temporal duration but timelessness, then eternal life belongs to those who live in the present.

Wittgenstein

Appendix: Thinking about Thinking

The following outline of some general features of consciousness did not seem appropriate to the body of this book, although
recognizing these features should enhance appreciation of
many points made in the text. Besides, the serious reader may
find it intellectually entertaining to be aware of some of the
general traits of thinking at the very moment that his own thinking can illustrate them.

Reflexivity. Beginning to think about thinking illustrates one of
its pervasive features—reflexivity. Every time you catch yourself
in the act, whether of thinking, feeling, seeing, wanting, or imagining, you are reflecting upon your own conscious state. You are
aware of being aware (of whatever you're aware of).

Reflection, in the sense I mean here, is not the peculiar prov-
ince of philosophers. Everybody reflects much of the time but,
unlike philosophers, not systematically. Animals and infants
probably don't reflect, but the rest of us do, whenever we realize
what we're doing. That's what reflecting is.

If you're clever and shrewd, it may have occurred to you that
to reflect upon what you're doing (thinking, feeling, or at this
moment reading) is itself to do something. Thus, while reflecting
makes you aware of what you're doing, it may compete with
what you're doing. So, reflection is not to be confused with concentration. It can be a distraction.

Reflection upon reflection is also possible. In fact, that's what
we're doing right now. To realize that you realize what you're
doing is to reflect at a second level. Then you are doubly re-
moved from what you're doing. That's one of the occupational
hazards of doing philosophy.

Ongoingness. Obviously, you are not conscious all the time. In
calling consciousness *ongoing,* I mean that there are no stops

in consciousness, even if there are stops *of* consciousness. Compare it with eating: when you are eating, you are not eating at every moment; but during any conscious duration, you are conscious at every moment. To say that consciousness is ongoing means that there are no stops in consciousness, even if there are different levels of consciousness. If it makes sense to speak of rates of consciousness, then we can speak of being conscious faster and faster or slower and slower. What this means, of course, is only that we can change the subject, what we are conscious of, rapidly or slowly. But to say that consciousness is ongoing is simply to say that even when you are blissfully focused on a single object of contemplation, still you are conscious. You may be totally relaxed and at peace, but your consciousness can never be still—unchanging, it goes on.

You may have noticed that in making these observations, reflecting was required. Therefore, at the time of reflection, consciousness is not only moving but changing, from unreflected to reflexive. You can never be conscious of being conscious of one thing without thereby being conscious of at least two things—the object of your awareness and your awareness itself.

Continuity. This is the feature implied on the phrase "stream of consciousness." Consciousness is a series of mental events, but the events in the series cannot be clearly divided up into distinct bits. This characteristic of consciousness is not due to the fact that reality is continuous, if that is a fact. For even if everything we are aware of were separate from everything else, still our consciousness of them would not be similarly divisible. Except for certain abrupt changes, the transition from being conscious of one thing to being conscious of another is generally a gradual process.

As you might have noticed, being conscious of the continuity of consciousness confirms the continuity of reflexive consciousness. Reflecting seems to straddle the state it is a reflection upon and the next state.

Horizonality. Ordinarily we refer to the visual horizon as the extent to which we *can* see. Let's extend the notion. Every visual experience has a limited scope. As I use the term, its *limit* or *boundary* is its horizon. The horizon is how far you *do* see at that moment. The boundaries change from moment to moment, as you move around and turn your head. Observe that you cannot see how far you can see. As soon as you peek out of the corner of your eye to see how far to the side you can see, you see

farther. You can see where the boundary was, but never where
it is.

The reason for changing horizons seems to be that at any
given moment, you focus on only part of what is there before
your eyes. The rest is vague and in the background. This is what
psychologists refer to as the *figure/ground* character of sight.
You always focus on something, and you're only hazily aware of
the rest. Naturally, then, you can never focus on the boundary of
the whole experience.

Scientific observation of eye movements indicates that the
change of focus is rapid and haphazard. Fortunately, we are able
to put it all together into a coherent picture. I suspect that part
of this ability to unify the parts is due to our limited capacity for
reflection. Evidently we can be reflexively aware only of what
we're focusing on, and then of but part of that. To see what I
mean, take a look around and try to catch yourself seeing what
you're seeing. You'll succeed some of the time, but normally your
eye movements will keep a step ahead of you.

In describing consciousness as horizonal, I mean that vision is
but a special case of a general phenomenon. What is true of
seeing is true of other modes of perceiving, imagining, remembering, and feeling (emotions). In general, your consciousness
has a limited scope and you can't focus on its limit without
extending the limit. This phenomenon is something like chasing
your shadow—you always come close, but you never succeed in
catching it.

Moreover, the contents of consciousness near the boundaries
(at a given moment) are not in focus. That means that to be aware
of being conscious (to be reflexively aware) of what is near the
boundaries requires putting it into focus. Thus, the boundaries
are changed, and what was in focus is no longer so. It may even
be out of the mental picture altogether.

To appreciate all this, simply reflect on your own awareness
right now. Try to keep track of what you're aware of. Whenever
you realize what it is, you'll realize that there is also something
else. When you realize what that is, you will no longer be aware
of what you were previously aware of. If you continue this reflexive process for a while, I'm sure you'll see what I've been trying
to describe. You'll realize that there is a lot more going on in
your consciousness than you realize. And you'll realize that no
matter how hard you try, your consciousness will always stay at
least a step ahead of your reflection.

Overlappingness. This characteristic of consciousness is connected with the previous ones. That is, a state of consciousness

may, and usually does, include some of what the previous state included. This feature is particularly related to the continuity of consciousness. Not only do conscious states merge into one another, making it difficult to speak of successive states, but their contents overlap.

Almost every experience illustrates this feature. An easy example is when your eyes pan across a scene: at each moment you see something you didn't see a moment before, you don't see something you did see a moment before, but you do see much of what you saw a moment before. Another example is listening to a melody. You don't hear a sequence of disconnected notes. On the other hand, you don't hear two successive notes simultaneously. However, when you hear each note, you hear it in conscious relation to the previous notes. Presumably the same sort of overlappingness applies to hearing a description or following an argument.

Reflection involves a special kind of overlapping. Here, one conscious state includes another, although the other may be destroyed in the process. For example, if you're aware of your experience of reading this sentence, your reading is included in being aware of it. And, maybe you were so aware of reading that you could no longer, for that moment, read.

Spontaneity. From what has been said so far, it should be obvious that your consciousness is not something you can control very much. Some people have the illusion of determining what comes into their minds, but it is clear that this is an illusion. The reason is simple: if you were to determine the contents of your consciousness in advance, you would have to be conscious of them in order to make that determination. But then, of course, the determination wouldn't be necessary, since in making it, you would have done already the very thing that it was the determination to do—to be conscious of some particular thing.

Naturally, you can call some of the shots. You can open or close your eyes. You can change the subject or pay attention. But the specific details of what is going on necessarily elude predetermination. That's what I mean by calling consciousness spontaneous.

A Note on the Unconscious

In the course of this book, I avoided the notion of the unconscious. For example, in making the point that you don't have everything under control (Chapter 5), I avoided the use of psy-

choanalytic concepts that refer to the unconscious, such as unconscious symbols, unconscious wishes, unconscious motives.
My reason was not to ignore the phenomena designated by
these terms but to make my point without assuming any particular psychological model, for example, the model of the psyche as
consisting of the conscious and the unconscious (or of the ego,
id, and superego). There are many phenomena related to the
notion of the unconscious, such as dreams, obsessions, fixa-
tions, and (ego) defenses. Though unmentioned, they may be
relevant to many aspects of our discussion, which may have
seemed to take on the naive appearance of assuming that all
problems and conditions can be readily handled by straightforward reflection on one's own states and patterns of consciousness. For example, I seemed to suggest that once you realize that
there is no "real self," you automatically give up the idea of
having a self-image (or at least of taking it too seriously), and no
longer have self-directed emotions such as pride and shame.
But, of course, it is not so simple as that. I don't pretend that it
is. I have not tried to produce a theory of human nature or an
account of all psychological phenomena. I've tried only to point
out certain things necessary to self-understanding.

I do have certain misgivings about the notion of the unconscious, at least as commonly conceived. It seems to be viewed
as a vast storehouse of thoughts and feelings (mostly unpleasant
ones, on some views) that the person is not conscious of. Occasionally, they come to the fore of consciousness, but mostly they
just lurk in the depths of the unconscious while having their
untold effects on the conscious.

All right, these ideas deserve more attention than I'm giving
them here, but without doing them justice, let me express my
basic misgiving about them. Now a thought or feeling is an
event. It either happens or it doesn't. If it does, it happens at a
certain time, for a certain duration. Similar states may occur at
other times. But there is no state that exists but does not occur.
On my view, all states are conscious states. But only some of
them are reflected upon. The rest are not. Those that are not
reflected upon occur without the person's being aware of their
occurrence. These are presumably what exponents of the unconscious refer to as unconscious states. What I object to, then, is
the idea that these states are lurking somewhere when they're
not actually occurring (it is not enough, on this view, that the
person be unaware of them when they do occur). Also, as you
might have guessed, I object to the idea that there is some place
where they are when they're lurking.

It seems to me that the phenomena supposed to be explained by the unconscious are perfectly real but that the explanation is gratuitous. There is no reason to think that unconscious states must be responsible for acts, thoughts, and feelings that a person cannot explain or justify to himself. For only states that occur can explain anything. Rather, what must be realized is that there are many things about one's mental life (and one's actions) that are *not* conscious. You don't know what's going on in your brain or how it works, but obviously it has much to do with your mental life. There are relationships between your thoughts and feelings that you may not be aware of. There are patterns in your behavior and in your moods that you may be unaware of or, if you are aware of them, that you are unable to explain. Your dreams, which are unconscious in the sense of not being reflected upon when they occur, may make little sense, although it is always possible to make (invent) sense of them that seems convincing. In short, all the why's you cannot figure out needn't be explained by a whole breed of hidden what's. This is not to say how they are to be explained, but only to rule out a certain type of appealing but gratuitous explanation.

To say that you don't know why you do the things you do is not to say that you have hidden reasons for them. There may, of course, be hidden causes.

For Further Reading

There follows a list of novels, plays, stories, and books and articles in philosophy, psychology, sociology, anthropology, and theology. They make up a diverse selection of readings on themes discussed in this book and on related themes as well. Needless to say, no endorsement is implied.

Part A is a brief list of texts and anthologies of general relevance. Part B is a more detailed list of works relating to topics discussed in particular chapters of this book. The necessarily brief descriptions are meant only to indicate how these writings are connected with themes in this book. As might be expected, items cited under one chapter are often relevant to others. Where possible, inexpensive paperback editions are cited.

Part A   General References

Barnes, Hazel E., *An Existentialist Ethics.* New York: Vintage, 1971.

> An attempt to extract an ethical position from an existentialist viewpoint. Not only dealing with existential philosophers, it considers recent developments in politics, Eastern philosophy, and theology.

Barrett, William, *Irrational Man.* New York: Anchor, 1962.

> A valuable and popular introduction to those writers generally labeled existential philosophers.

Greening, Thomas C. (ed.), *Existential Humanistic Psychology.* Belmont, Calif.: Brooks/Cole, 1971.

> A short anthology representing the so-called Third Force movement in psychology.

94

Heidegger, Martin, *Being and Time.* New York: Harper & Row, 1962.

The classic existentialist treatise. This difficult, massive work analyzes the notion of "being in the world" and care as its basic mode, and provides an account of the existential–ontological structure of temporality. The style and the idiosyncratic terminology, not to mention the ideas themselves, render it nearly inaccessible.

Karl, Frederick R., and Leo Hamalian (eds.), *The Existential Imagination.* Greenwich, Conn.: Fawcett, 1963.

A superb anthology of existentialist themes expressed in short literary form.

Kaufmann, Walter (ed.), *Existentialism from Dostoevsky to Sartre.* New York: Meridian, 1956.

A popular selection of fictional and philosophical writings in the existentialist tradition. It contains a valuable introduction by the editor.

Sartre, Jean-Paul, "Existentialism is a Humanism," in *Existentialism and Human Emotions.* New York: Philosophical Library, 1957.

Sartre's informal account of what existentialism is and isn't. He explains the formula, "Existence precedes essence," and discusses freedom, subjectivism, and morality.

Sartre, Jean-Paul, *Being and Nothingness.* New York: Washington Square Press, 1966.

Sartre's famous treatise on the nature of consciousness (for itself). This long, rambling work contains insightful observations on human existence, but it lacks the style of Sartre's literary works. Translator Hazel E. Barnes's excellent introduction guides the reader to the landmarks of the labyrinth.

Warnock, Mary, *Existentialism.* Oxford: Oxford University Press, 1970.

A compact survey of existentialist thinkers from Kierkegaard and Nietzsche to Sartre and Merleau-Ponty. While special attention is paid to the phenomenological methods of Husserl and their influence, the author's analytic perspective makes the book particularly interesting.

Part B   Related Reading by Chapter

Chapter 1

Barth, John, *The Floating Opera.* New York: Bantam, 1972.

A novelistic counterpart to Camus's *Myth of Sisyphus,* dealing with a life of growing meaninglessness and with suicide as a possible solution.

Beckett, Samuel, *Waiting for Godot.* New York: Grove, 1954.

————, *Endgame.* New York: Grove, 1958.

Two classic absurdist plays. Godot is whom the characters are waiting for, not that he will show up, not that he exists, not that it matters. *Endgame* is a similarly bleak scene of empty lives playing out the comic game of existence, in which the trivial is as significant as anything else.

Camus, Albert, *The Myth of Sisyphus.* New York: Vintage, 1959.

The definitive essay on the absurd. The absurdity of life is the premise. The question is, "Does suicide follow?" The suggested answer is, "No, suicide is only surrendering to the absurd." Instead, Camus advocates a life of conscious, passionate defiance of the absurd. He illustrates his position with references to numerous literary figures.

Camus, Albert, *The Stranger.* New York: Vintage, 1960.

An immensely popular story of a man living without purpose. His emotionless life leads to a pointless murder, and feeling stirs (one of rebirth) only on the day of execution.

Dostoevsky, Fyodor, *The Brothers Karamazov.* Baltimore: Penguin, 1958.

The masterpiece of tender-hearted vs. hard-headed mentalities. The famous scene of the Grand Inquisitor (reprinted in *The Existential Imagination,* cited in Part A) deals with the value of blind faith and submission to external authority.

Dostoevsky, Fyodor, *Notes from Underground.* New York: Signet, 1961.

The tortured reflections of a hopelessly alienated man, for whom no reason for doing anything is every reason for doing nothing.

Eliade, Mircea, *Myth and Reality*. New York: Harper Torchbooks, 1968.

A fascinating view of the functions and structures of myths. The author is able to identify and integrate themes from an incredible range of human experiences.

Frankl, Victor, *Man's Search for Meaning*. New York: Pocket Books, 1963.

The development of logotherapy, a type of existential psychoanalysis, out of the horror of Nazi concentration camps. Moving, indeed, is the story of those who could find meaning and hope in such circumstances—and of those who couldn't.

Heller, Joseph, *Catch 22*. New York: Dell, 1970.

A hilariously serious account of institutional insanity, illustrated by, but not limited to, the military. "Am I crazy?" is no easy question to answer in such a context.

Hemingway, Ernest, *The Old Man and the Sea*. New York: Scribners, 1962.

The story illustrates how meaning can be found in the context of a person's own choosing.

Kafka, Franz, *The Castle*. New York: Modern Library, 1969.

———, *The Trial*. New York: Vintage, 1969.

Two novels of the absurd. In each, the protagonist faces a world that, despite his tireless efforts, continually eludes his comprehension. His every act of will only underlines his helplessness. He is guilty only of being there.

Matson, Wallace, *The Existence of God*. Ithaca, N.Y.: Cornell University Press, 1965.

An exhaustive critical examination of arguments for the existence of God.

Nagel, Thomas, "The Absurd," in *Journal of Philosophy,* LXVIII (1971), pp. 716–27.

An analytic philosopher's attempt to unravel the idea and the experience of the absurd. He seems to conclude that the sense of the absurd is predicated on a demand for an unreasonable sort of meaning.

Pavese, Cesare, "Suicides," in *The Existential Imagination,* Karl and Hamalian, pp. 244–59.

An account of a man succumbing to death in life. He is aware of the absurdity of his life and of the meaninglessness of his relationship with a certain woman. Even when trying to live, he cannot exist without guilt.

Russell, Bertrand, "A Free Man's Worship," in *Mysticism and Logic.* New York: Anchor, 1957, pp. 44–54.

An extraordinarily eloquent statement of the meaning of life in a "world of fact." In a world stripped of illusion, there is still room for love of truth, appreciation of beauty, and the dignity of man.

Sartre, Jean-Paul, *Nausea.* New York: New Directions, 1964.

The story of a historian whose life, professional and otherwise, is devoid of meaning. Triviality is the hallmark of his work, silent indifference the hallmark of his world.

Tillich, Paul, *The Dynamics of Faith.* New York: Harper Torchbooks, 1958.

A systematic account of faith taken as "ultimate concern." Ultimate concern is held to be necessary for an integrated, "centered" personality. Be that as it may, the question remains, "Is ultimate concern justified?"

de Unamuno, Miguel, "Saint Emmanuel the Good, Martyr," in *The Existential Imagination,* Karl and Hamalian, pp. 97–132.

A benign version of Dostoevsky's Grand Inquisitor. The question is the same, "Are people best off with blind faith?"

Wittgenstein, Ludwig, *Tractatus Logico-Philosophicus.* London: Routledge & Kegan Paul, 1961.

A notoriously difficult book on the relation of words and things and on the nature and limits of language in general. Relevant to our purposes are the concluding passages on life and on what cannot be said, for example, "When the answer cannot be put into words, neither can the question be put into words."

Chapter 2

Beckett, Samuel, "The Expelled," in *The Existential Imagination,* Karl and Hamalian, pp. 217–229.

Of a man whose alienation from the world of people and things is total. In his isolation, he can focus only on meaningless details.

Dostoevsky, Fyodor, *Notes from Underground*. New York: Signet, 1961.

This book is worth citing again (see Chapter 1). The Underground Man is isolated from others by virtue of his own morbid reflections. His recognition of the sham of society renders him both contemptuous and envious of humanity.

Feuerbach, Ludwig, *The Essence of Christianity*. New York: Harper Torchbooks, 1957.

An illustration of the concept of alienation as misidentification. For Feuerbach, the essence of religion is the essence of man himself projected outside himself and reified or personified.

Fromm, Erich, *The Art of Loving*. New York: Bantam, 1963.

A psychological account of love not as romantic renunciation of oneself in another, but as the highest form of self-assertion.

James, William, *The Varieties of Religious Experience*. New York: Collier, 1961.

The chapter on mysticism provides a good source of first person descriptions of mystical experiences.

Marx, Karl, *Economic and Philosophical Manuscripts,* in T. B. Bottomore (ed.), *Karl Marx Early Writings*. New York: McGraw-Hill, 1964.

Includes Marx's account of the alienation of labor and other forms of alienation as well. Alienation is the projection of human powers onto outside objects, such as capital and the state, and the subsequent identification with those objects.

Pappenheim, Fritz, *The Alienation of Modern Man*. New York: Monthly Review Press, 1959.

A political and sociological analysis of alienation and its causes. The author sees alienation as rooted in the social order. Hence, it can be overcome only by transforming that order.

Riesman, David, *The Lonely Crowd*. New Haven: Yale University Press, 1950.

A sociological account of alienation in American society, based on the now famous concepts of inner- and other-directedness.

Sartre, Jean-Paul, *No Exit.* New York: Vintage, 1955.
Sartre's most famous play, whose characters sustain themselves by torturing each other, thus hellishly building on their mutual alienation.

Wilson, Colin, *The Outsider.* New York: Delta, 1967.
An extensive analysis of alienation in the lives and writings of famous writers and artists. On the freedom and frightfulness of seeing more deeply.

Chapter 3

Aichinger, Ilse, "The Bound Man," in *The Existential Imagination,* Karl and Hamalian, pp. 276–288.
Of a man who awakens to find himself bound in ropes. He becomes the Bound Man for others, as he does remarkable things (for a man bound in ropes), instead of choosing to be free and anonymous.

Goffman, Erving, *The Presentation of Self in Everyday Life.* New York: Anchor, 1959.
A sociological account of play-acting and role-playing in ordinary situations.

Kafka, Franz, *The Metamorphosis.* New York: Modern Library, 1952.
When a man awakens to find himself transformed into what looks like a giant insect, there is, needless to say, a definite conflict between what he is for himself and what he is for others.

Kierkegaard, Sören, *Fear and Trembling.* New York: Anchor, 1954.
Among other things (including one version of what the absurd is), an account of different types of defining relations, which, like Tillich's concept of ultimate concern, illustrates what I pejoratively call overidentification.

Laing, R. D., *The Divided Self.* Baltimore: Penguin, 1965.
A sensitive and profound analysis of schizoid and schizophrenic conditions. The concepts of ontological insecurity and of the false self make these conditions intelligible. Gives many examples of self-alienation.

Lawrence, D. H., *Women in Love.* New York: Viking, 1960.

A novel (Lawrence's favorite) of alienation from society and from self. It deals, in part, with finding oneself and being oneself with others.

de l'Isle-Adam, Villier, "The Desire to Be a Man," in *The Existential Imagination,* Karl and Hamalian, pp. 88–96.

Of an aged actor who has identified only with the characters he has played. Devoid of feelings of his own, he makes a desperate attempt to generate some anyway.

Miller, Arthur, *Death of a Salesman.* New York: Viking, 1971.

A drama of the totally other-directed man. When he outlives his acceptability to others, he finds that he has nothing left.

Moravia, Alberto, "Back to the Sea," in *The Existential Imagination,* Karl and Hamalian, pp. 230–243.

The story of a man embedded in both sorts of self-aliena tion. There are parts of himself that he cannot identify with, and parts of his past that he cannot disidentify with.

Chapter 4

Bugental, James F. T., "The Self: Process or Illusion?" in *Existential Humanistic Psychology,* Greening, pp. 55–71.

If the Self is but one's history, then what remains is the "I-process," as the author calls it. Recognizing the latter is the key to transcending the former.

Erikson, Erik, *Identity: Youth and Crisis.* New York: Norton, 1968.

A psychoanalytic view of the human life-cycle, with emphasis on the late adolescent stage, by the coiner of the phrase "identity crisis."

Hesse, Hermann, *Steppenwolf.* New York: Bantam, 1969.

The immensely popular story of a man with at least two sides, and possibly a thousand. The key to his self-realization is his recognition that there is no one thing that he has to be.

Hume, David, "Personal Identity," in *A Treatise of Nature.* Oxford: Oxford University Press, 1955.

The Western equivalent of the Buddhist doctrine of no-self. Hume finds himself unable to find himself and concludes that there is nothing to be found, save the stream of experiences called his by virtue of their connection in memory.

Kant, Immanuel, "Transcendental Deduction," in *Critique of Pure Reason,* 2nd edition. New York: St. Martin's Press, 1965, pp. 151–175.

Very roughly speaking (Kant is difficult enough to explain without taking him out of context), Kant's position is that the self (transcendental ego) is not an object, hence not to be experienced, but the basic principle of unity of experience. He later argues, in the "Second Analogy of Experience," that what I call the "sense of self" is possible only if objects are conceived of as distinct from oneself.

Maslow, Abraham, *Toward a Psychology of Being.* New York: Van Nostrand, 1968.

On self-actualization as the creative fulfillment of one's potentialities. The self is not a static entity but an evolving process.

May, Rollo, *Man's Search for Himself.* New York: Signet, 1967.

An examination of modern-day anxiety and a proposal for overcoming it. The author defines the idea of a free, creative, integrated personality as the positive side to the awareness that began with anxiety and loneliness.

Mead, George Herbert, *Mind, Self, and Society.* Chicago: University of Chicago Press, 1934.

The social psychologist's view of self as essentially a social object. This concept, along with that of "the generalized other," is useful for scientific purposes ("symbolic interactionism"), as is role theory. But the question remains whether a person's own self-conception should be limited to his social self.

Needleman, Jacob (trans.), *Being-in-the-World.* New York: Harper Torchbooks, 1968.

A translation of the major papers of Ludwig Binswanger on existential psychoanalysis. The translator provides an excellent account of the concept of "the existential a priori," which refers to a person's fundamental ways of structuring and relating to the world, thereby characterizing his particular sense of self.

Piaget, Jean, and Bärbel Inhelder, *The Psychology of the Child.* New York: Harper Torchbooks, 1969.

A summary of the Swiss psychologist Piaget's career of experimental and theoretical work in developmental cognitive psychology. With his collaborator, Inhelder, Piaget describes the child's pattern of acquiring basic concepts for structuring the world and his relationship to it.

Sartre, Jean-Paul, *The Transcendence of the Ego.* New York: Noonday, 1957.

A critique of Husserl's concept of the transcendental ego. The discussion of the "I" and the "Me" parallels (in certain respects) the subject–object distinction I use in this book.

Shoemaker, Sidney, "Self-Reference and Self-Awareness," in *Journal of Philosophy,* LXV (1968), pp. 555–67.

An analytic philosopher's account of the use of "I" as subject and its use as object. He argues that the second is logically dependent on the first, a position paralleling my view that having a self-image depends on having a sense of self.

Strawson, P. F., *Individuals.* New York: Anchor, 1963.

The first chapter, "Bodies," establishes material objects as primary objects of reference, but the third chapter, "Persons," recognizes persons also as primary. The author argues that a person is essentially subject *and* object, and that an idea of oneself requires the idea of others.

Watts, Alan, *The Book.* New York: Vintage, 1972.

A popularistic account of the self as not a thing but as essentially part of the world. Your skin is an arbitrary dividing line, so the world is your body.

Chapter 5

Camus, Albert, *Caligula.* New York: Vintage, 1958.

Of a king whose assertion of freedom consists in the arbitrary domination of others—they are his thing.

Castañeda, Carlos, *The Teachings of Don Juan.* New York: Ballantine, 1968.

——, *A Separate Reality.* New York: Simon and Schuster, 1971.

———, *Journey to Ixtlan.* New York: Simon and Schuster, 1972.
  A fascinating account of the Yaqui sorcerer's teachings and practices. It is interesting to observe the author's growing appreciation of his teacher's idea of "seeing" beyond the ordinary world of categories and expectations. A remarkable idea of freedom is implied.

Fromm, Erich, *Escape from Freedom.* New York: Avon, 1965.
  A psychosocial examination of modern man's tendency to submit to authority rather than to assert his own.

Krishnamurti, J., *Think on These Things.* New York: Perennial Library, 1970.
  The sage's thoughts on many things, including the concept of attention as opposed to concentration, as the way of finding the present.

Laing, R. D., *The Politics of Experience.* New York: Ballantine, 1968.
  An impassioned outcry against the repression of experience, and a plea for the freedom of experience in a variety of contexts.

Lao-tzu, *The Way of Life.* New York: Capricorn, 1962.
  The mystical, but practical, philosophy of Taoism, emphasizing freedom through experiencing and harmonizing oneself with one's surroundings.

Lucretius, *On the Nature of the Universe.* Baltimore: Penguin, 1951.
  A poetic statement of the much misunderstood philosophy of hedonism, which is more serene than sensational.

Aurelius, Marcus, *Meditations.* Baltimore: Penguin, 1964.
  The aphorisms of stoicism, a philosophy that is not as fatalistic or as passive as it seems.

Nietzsche, Friedrich, *Beyond Good and Evil.* Chicago: Gateway, 1955.
  Freedom through transcendence of the "herd morality." Contrary to popular opinion, Nietzsche is a humanist, not a nihilist.

Sartre, Jean-Paul, "Bad Faith," *Being and Nothingness,* I, 2, pp. 86–116.

——, "The Room," in *The Existential Imagination,* Karl and Hamalian, pp. 192–216.

> Sartre's account of this well-known notion is illustrated in a story of an insane man, his wife, and his in-laws. The question is, "Who is guilty of bad faith and who is true to himself?"

Sennett, Richard. *The Uses of Disorder.* New York: Vintage, 1970.

> A sociologist's proposal for building happenstance and randomness into city planning.

Vizinczey, Stephen, *The Rules of Chaos.* New York: McCall, 1969.

> Showing that events are determined largely not by human decision but by chance. Hence, it is folly to think that one is in control of his destiny, or that mankind is in control of its.

Voltaire, Francois, *Candide.* New York: Signet, 1961.

> A delightful story of how to run your luck on the assumption that this is the best of all possible worlds (whether it is a good one is another question).

Watts, Alan, *The Wisdom of Insecurity.* New York: Pantheon, 1952.

> How to go beyond anxiety, not by eliminating its conditions (danger, uncertainty, purposelessness), but by making something positive out of them. The basic idea is to return to the present.

Appendix

Husserl, Edmund, *The Phenomenology of Internal Time-Consciousness.* Bloomington, Ind.: Indiana University Press, 1964.

> A fascinating but difficult examination of the many temporal aspects of consciousness.

MacIntyre, A. C., *The Unconscious.* London: Routledge & Kegan Paul, 1958.

> A philosophical examination of this commonly used psychological concept.